Declaration

Lindsay Anderson

Kenneth Tynan

Stuart Holroyd

John Osborne

DECLARATION

Doris Lessing

Colin Wilson

Bill Hopkins

John Wain

EDITED BY

TOM MASCHLER

Readers Union: LONDON 1959
MacGibbon and Kee

© MACGIBBON & KEE

This RU edition was produced in 1959 for sale to its members
only by Readers Union Ltd at 38 William IV Street, Charing
Cross, London, W.C.2, and at Letchworth Garden City, Hert-
fordshire. Full details of membership may be obtained from our
London address. The book has been set in 10 on 12 point Pilgrim
and has been printed at the St Ann's Press, Altrincham. It was
first published in 1957 by MacGibbon & Kee.

Contents

Introduction

A NUMBER of young and widely opposed
writers have burst upon the scene and are striving to change many
of the values which have held good in recent years. No critic has
yet succeeded in assessing them or correlating them *objectively*
one to another. This volume aims at helping the public to understand what is happening while it is actually happening—at uncovering a certain pattern taking shape in British thought and
literature.

Recently the *Daily Mail* went so far as to warn people, a few
weeks before the publication of a young author's first book, that
they were about to be beset by ' a new espresso evangelist, another
seer of the Soup Kitchens, a fresh messiah of the milk bars . . .!'
Meanwhile the ' serious' critic who occupies his time playing
literary crossword puzzles and comparing every other novel to
L∗*c*∗*y J*∗*m*, commits an equal disservice to literature in another
direction. The apparent inability of critics to grasp the plain sense
of what they have before them cannot be illustrated more poin-
tedly than by quoting a leader of *The Times Literary Supple-
ment*. We are gravely told that 'we live in a muffled age . . .' in
which ' a combined mood of rather damp and grey moderation and
rather complicatedly motivated aggressive hysteria is likely, perhaps, for some time to remain the typical mood of many of our
cleverest young writers.' It would be difficult to demonstrate
more clearly that 'muffling' has produced a chain reaction. The
piece is entitled ' Sense and Sensibility '.

We have to thank an even lower level of journalism for the
phrase ' Angry Young Men ' which has been employed to group,
without so much as an attempt at understanding, all those sharing
a certain indignation against the apathy, the complacency, the
idealistic bankruptcy of their environment. Thus the writers who
have set themselves the task of waking us up have been rendered
harmless in the A.Y.M. cage. However, despite the strenuous efforts

of the Press to create hostility through constant misrepresentations, these writers have found an audience, and their anger has proved a highly saleable commodity. To be prejudiced against them purely because they are angry is to imagine naïvely that anger is the sole substance of their work ('Yes, Mr Osborne is a very clever playwright; such a pity he's an Angry Young Man'). The label has become so ubiquitous that even Mr Nigel Dennis, the author of *Cards of Identity*, although named as an A.Y.M., turns out to be over forty, the father of teen-age children, and the mildest of men.

It is important to note that although most of the contributors to this volume have at some time or other been termed Angry Young Men they do *not* belong to a united movement. Far from it; they attack one another directly or indirectly in these pages. Some were even reluctant to appear between the same covers with others whose views they violently oppose. The fact that they have overcome their hesitation is in itself an indication of genuine belief.

Declaration is a collection of separate positions. The contributors are principally concerned with expressing themselves in their own particular fields, and here, in their credos, they define their positions in relation to society today. They are attempting in their own way to create, to lead.

We must remember that they are in their twenties and thirties; they will develop and may even change their ideas. This is a prerogative of any creative artist. A writer is a constantly gathering force, and I believe that he should not be judged on such an ephemeral standard as a single book. He should be viewed not only within the society around him but within the context of a whole lifetime's work. Thus the man dominates his work, and his beliefs are all-important.

That the contributors to this book should be prepared to commit themselves to the extent of condensing their beliefs into a few thousand words reveals a common sense of urgency. Clearly they have blatantly exposed themselves, and these statements offer a magnificent target which may well prove irresistible to critics.

It would have been easy to reply as Mr Kingsley Amis did, when invited to join this company. He wrote : ' I hate all this pharisaical twittering about the " state of our civilization " and I suspect anyone who wants to buttonhole me about my " rôle in society ".

This book is likely to prove a valuable addition to the cult of the Solemn Young Man; I predict a great success for it.' I am surprised, in the light of the able Fabian pamphlet Mr Amis penned, that he should be so reticent about a writer's rôle in society.

If *Declaration* can provide readers with an insight into the minds of some of our writers of today who may determine our society tomorrow, it will have achieved its aim. We can accept or reject, but we *cannot* afford to dismiss, these writers. I am only sorry that the book could not include the many other young writers who feel they have something of importance to say.

TOM MASCHLER

Doris Lessing

Born in Persia, 1919. In 1924 her father bought a maize farm in Southern Rhodesia. Educated at the Roman Catholic Convent School in Salisbury for five years, and for one year at the girls' High School. Her mother wanted her to be a pianist, and it was a shock when, in Doris Lessing's own words, 'I discovered suddenly that I had no talent whatsoever.' Left school at fourteen. Started writing at eighteen and composed and destroyed six novels. From 1943, upon her second marriage, was busy politically taking her first lesson from Communists and Socialists in the R.A.F. For the first time in her life she met people who were prepared to do more about the colour bar than deplore it. 1949: came to England and her novel *The Grass is Singing* was published. A brilliant success. 1950: *This Was the Old Chief's Country*. 1952: *Martha Quest*, the first of five volumes called *The Children of Violence*, was followed in 1954 by the second, *A Proper Marriage*. 1953: *Five*, short novels. 1954: she was awarded the Somerset Maugham Prize. 1956: *Retreat to Innocence*, a novel. 1957: *Going Home*, a travel book. She says, 'England seems to me the ideal country to live in because it is quiet and unstimulating and leaves you in peace.'

To say, in 1957, that one believes artis should be committed, is to arouse hostility and distrust because the quantities of bad novels, pictures and films produced under t banner of committedness; also because of a current mood of rea tion against socialist art-jargon, the words and phrases of whic have been debased by a parrot-use by the second-rate to a poi where many of us suffer from a nervous reluctance to use the at all. The reaction is so powerful and so prompt that one has on to stand up on a public platform and say that one still believes the class analysis of society and therefore of art, in short that on is a marxist, for nine-tenths of the audience immediately to assun that one believes novels should be simple tracts about factories strikes or economic injustice.

I see no reason why good writers should not, if they have a bei that way, write angry protest novels about economic injustic Many good writers have. Dickens, for instance, was often inspire by poverty and injustice. Novels like *Germinal* or *The Jungle* are n to be despised. A writer's natural talent may drive him to transforr what might have been a simple morality-tale into something muc more powerful. Or his talent may be adequate only for crude pr test. But propagandist literature, religious or political, is as old a literature itself, and has sometimes been good and sometimes bac

Recently it has been very bad; and that is why the idea of com mittedness is in disrepute. But at least it is in debate, and that i a good thing: passionate polemics about art or about anythin else are always a sign of health.

Polemics about art now must take into account what has hap pened in the communist countries where socialist theories of ar have been put into practice. The 'agonized reappraisals' that are going on everywhere in the socialist movements are a seminal force; for I do not believe that humanity is so compartmented that

reappraisals, agonized or not, can go on in one section of it and not quickly and usefully influence anybody who thinks at all.

As a writer I am concerned first of all with novels and stories, though I believe that the arts continuously influence each other, and that what is true of one art in any given epoch is likely to be true of the others. I am concerned that the novel and the story should not decline as art-forms any further than they have from the high peak of literature; that they should possibly regain their greatness. For me the highest point of literature was the novel of the nineteenth century, the work of Tolstoy, Stendhal, Dostoevsky, Balzac, Turgenev, Chekhov; the work of the great realists. I define realism as art which springs so vigorously and naturally from a strongly-held, though not necessarily intellectually-defined, view of life that it absorbs symbolism. I hold the view that the realist novel, the realist story, is the highest form of prose writing; higher than and out of the reach of any comparison with expressionism, impressionism, symbolism, naturalism or any other ism.

The great men of the nineteenth century had neither religion nor politics nor aesthetic principles in common. But what they did have in common was a climate of ethical judgement; they shared certain values; they were humanists. A nineteenth-century novel is recognizably a nineteenth-century novel because of this moral climate.

If there is one thing which distinguishes our literature, it is a confusion of standards and the uncertainty of values. It would be hard, now, for a writer to use Balzacian phrases like 'sublime virtue' or 'monster of wickedness' without self-consciousness. Words, it seems, can no longer be used simply and naturally. All the great words like love, hate; life, death; loyalty, treachery; contain their opposite meanings and half a dozen shades of dubious implication. Words have become so inadequate to express the richness of our experience that the simplest sentence overheard on a bus reverberates like words shouted against a cliff. One certainty we all accept is the condition of being uncertain and insecure. It is hard to make moral judgements, to use words like good and bad.

Yet I re-read Tolstoy, Stendhal, Balzac, and the rest of the old giants continuously. So do most of the people I know, people who

The small personal voice

DORIS LESSING

are left and right, committed and uncommitted, religious and un-religious, but who have at least this in common, that they read novels as I think they should be read, for illumination, in order to enlarge one's perception of life.

Why? Because we are in search of certainties? Because we want a return to a comparatively uncomplicated world? Because it gives us a sense of safety to hear Balzac's thundering verdicts of guilt or innocence, and to explore with Dostoevsky, for instance in *Crime and Punishment*, the possibilities of moral anarchy, only to find order restored at the end with the simplest statements of faith in forgiveness, expiation, redemption?

Recently I finished reading an American novel which pleased me; it was witty, intelligent, un-self-pitying, courageous. Yet when I put it down I knew I would not re-read it. I asked myself why not, what demand I was making on the author that he did not answer. Why was I left dissatisfied with nearly all the contem-porary novels I read? Why, if I were reading for my own needs, rather than for the purposes of informing myself about what was going on, would I begin re-reading *War and Peace* or *The Red and the Black*?

Put directly, like this, the answer seemed to me clear. I was not looking for a firm re-affirmation of old ethical values, many of which I don't accept; I was not in search of the pleasures of familiarity. I was looking for the warmth, the compassion, the humanity, the love of people which illuminates the literature of the nineteenth century and which makes all these old novels a statement of faith in man himself.

These are qualities which I believe are lacking from literature now.

This is what I mean when I say that literature should be com-mitted. It is these qualities which I demand, and which I believe spring from being committed; for one cannot be committed with-out belief.

Committed to what? Not to being a propagandist for any poli-tical party. I never have thought so. I see no reason why writers should not work, in their rôle as citizens, for a political party; but they should never allow themselves to feel obliged to publicize any party policy or 'line' unless their own private passionate need as writers makes them do so : in which case the passion might, if they have talent enough, make literature of the propaganda.

Once a writer has a feeling of responsibility, as a human being, for the other human beings he influences, it seems to me he must become a humanist, and must feel himself as an instrument of change for good or for bad. That image of the pretty singer in the ivory tower has always seemed to me a dishonest one. Logically he should be content to sing to his image in the mirror. The act of getting a story or a novel published is an act of communication, an attempt to impose one's personality and beliefs on other people. If a writer accepts this responsibility, he must see himself, to use the socialist phrase, as an architect of the soul, and it is a phrase which none of the old nineteenth-century novelists would have shied away from.

But if one is going to be an architect, one must have a vision to build towards, and that vision must spring from the nature of the world we live in.

We are living at a time which is so dangerous, violent, explosive and precarious that it is in question whether soon there will be people left alive to write books and to read them. It is a question of life and death for all of us; and we are haunted, all of us, by the threat that even if some madman does not destroy us all, our children may be born deformed or mad. We are living at one of the great turning-points of history. In the last two decades man has made an advance as revolutionary as when he first got off his belly and stood upright. Yesterday, we split the atom. We assaulted that colossal citadel of power, the tiny unit of the substance of the universe. And because of this, the great dream and the great nightmare of centuries of human thought have taken flesh and walk beside us all, day and night. Artists are the traditional interpreters of dreams and nightmares, and this is no time to turn our backs on our chosen responsibilities, which is what we should be doing if we refused to share in the deep anxieties, terrors and hopes of human beings everywhere.

What is the choice before us? It is not merely a question of preventing an evil, but of strengthening a vision of a good which may defeat the evil.

Even before we liberated the power in the atom, so socialist economists claim, the products of our labour (that is, if freed from the artificial restrictions of a strangling economic system) were enough to feed and clothe all the people in the world; humanity could have been freed from want and drudgery if we had taken the brakes off the machines and if so much of the wealth we produced had not been spent on the engines of war. Even before we split the atom, the old dream of man liberated from the tyrannies of hunger and of cold had the solidity of something possible.

But to imagine free man, leisured man, is to step outside what we are. There is no one on this earth who is not twisted by fear and insecurity, and the compromises of thinking made inevitable by want and fear. Those people who see leisured man in terms of football matches and television-watching; those who say: ' You can't give man leisure, he won't know how to use it,' are as much victims of a temporary phase of economic development as the coupon-fillers and the screen-dreamers. Their imaginations are in bond to their own necessities. Slaves can envy the free; slaves can fight to free their children; but slaves suddenly set free are marked by the habits of submission; and slaves imagining freedom see it through the eyes of slaves.

I am convinced that we all stand at an open door, and that there is a new man about to be born, who has never been twisted by drudgery; a man whose pride as a man will not be measured by his capacity to shoulder work and responsibilities which he detests, which bore him, which are too small for what he could be; a man whose strength will not be gauged by the values of the mystique of suffering.

The imagination of the world already rejects hunger and poverty. We all believe they can be abolished. If humanity submits to living below the level of what is possible, it will be as shameful as when a human being chooses to live below the level of what he can be; or a nation falls below itself.

There are only two choices: that we force ourselves into the effort of imagination necessary to become what we are capable of being; or that we submit to being ruled by the office-boys of big business, or the socialist bureacrats who have forgotten that socialism means a desire for goodness and compassion—and the end of submission is that we shall blow ourselves up.

It is because it is so hard to think ourselves into the possibilities of the ancient dream of free man that the nightmare is so strong. Everyone in the world now, has moments when he throws down a newspaper, turns off the radio, shuts his ears to the man on the platform, and holds out his hand and looks at it, shaken with terror. The hand of a white man, held to the warmth of a northern indoor fire; the hand of a black man, held into the strong heat of the sun : we look at our working hands, brown and white, and then at the flat surface of a wall, the cold material of a city pavement, at breathing soil, trees, flowers, growing corn. We think : the tiny units of the matter of my hand, my flesh, are shared with walls, tables, pavements, trees, flowers, soil . . . and suddenly, and at any moment, a madman may throw a switch, and flesh and soil and leaves may begin to dance together in a flame of destruction. We are all of us made kin with each other and with everything in the world because of the kinship of possible destruction. And the history of the last fifty years does not help us to disbelieve in the possibility of a madman in a position of power. We are haunted by the image of an idiot hand, pressing down a great black lever; or a thumb pressing a button, as the dance of fiery death begins in one country and spreads over the earth; and above the hand the concentrated fanatic stare of a mad sick face.

Even the vision of the madman is not so bad. We are all of us, at times, this madman. Most of us have said, at some time or another, exhausted with the pressure of living, ' Oh for God's sake, press the button, turn down the switch, we've all had enough.' Because we can understand the madman, since he is part of us, we can deal with him, he is not so frightening as that other image : of a young empty-faced technician in anonymous overalls, saying Yes sir! and pressing the button. The anonymous technician, one of the growing army manning the departments of death, has no responsibility. He might turn the switch looking over his shoulder for confirmation at the Chairman of the Committee who ordered him to do it. And the Committee to another Committee. And the Chairman of that final superior Committee, one of those little half-men that we see on the news-reels, with their self-consciously democratic faces—that Chairman will say : ' I represent the people.' And the people is the brown man sitting under a tree, holding out the flesh of his forearm to the heat of the sun, thinking that the warmth of the great sun is the warmth also of that final blast of heat; the people is me.

Now, in March 1957, the British Government decides to continue the hydrogen bomb tests which threaten unborn children. Yet of the men who took the decision I am sure there is not one who says: Because of me thousands of children will be born crippled, blind, deaf, mad. They are members of a committee. They have no responsibility as individuals. They represent me. But I repudiate their act. I don't know one person, have never known a person, who would agree, as an individual, to throw that particular switch which will make children be born monsters. We all know there is a terrible gap between the public and the private conscience, and that until we bridge it we will never be safe from the murderous madman or the anonymous technician. But what is the nature of that gap? Partly, I think, it is that we have been so preoccupied with death and fear that we have not tried to imagine what living might be without the pressure of suffering. And the artists have been so busy with the nightmare they have had no time to re-write the old utopias. All our nobilities are those of the victories over suffering. We are soaked in the grandeur of suffering; and can imagine happiness only as the yawn of a suburban Sunday afternoon.

Yet there have been attempts enough to fill the gap. The literary products of the socialist third of the world can scarcely be said to lack optimism. Anyone who has studied them is familiar with that jolly, jaunty, curiously unemotional novel about the collective farm, the factory, the five-year plan, which is reminiscent of nothing so much as of a little boy whistling in the dark. The simple demand for simple statements of faith produces art so intolerably dull and false that one reads it yawning and returns to Tolstoy.

Meanwhile, the best and most vital works of Western literature have been despairing statements of emotional anarchy. If the typical product of communist literature during the last two decades is the cheerful little tract about economic advance, then the type of Western literature is the novel or play which one sees or reads with a shudder of horrified pity for all of humanity. If writers like Camus, Sartre, Genet, Beckett, feel anything but a tired pity for human beings, then it is not evident from their work.

I believe that the pleasurable luxury of despair, the acceptance of disgust, is as much a betrayal of what a writer should be as the acceptance of the simple economic view of man; both are aspects of cowardice, both fallings-away from a central vision, the two easy escapes of our time into false innocence. They are the opposite sides of the same coin. One sees man as the isolated individual unable to communicate, helpless and solitary; the other as collective man with a collective conscience. Somewhere between these two, I believe, is a resting-point, a place of decision, hard to reach and precariously balanced. It is a balance which must be continuously tested and reaffirmed. Living in the midst of this whirlwind of change, it is impossible to make final judgements or absolute statements of value. The point of rest should be the writer's recognition of man, the responsible individual, voluntarily submitting his will to the collective, but never finally; and insisting on making his own personal and private judgements before every act of submission.

I think that a writer who has for many years been emotionally involved in the basic ethical conflict of communism—what is due to the collective and what to the individual conscience—is peculiarly equipped to write of the dangers inherent in being ' committed'. The writer who can be bludgeoned into silence by fear or economic pressure is not worth considering; these problems are simple and the dangers easily recognizable. What is dangerous is the inner loyalty to something felt as something much greater than one's self. I remember, in Moscow, when this question was discussed, a writer replied to an accusation of being bludgeoned by the Party into false writing by saying: ' No one bludgeons us. Our conscience is at the service of the people. We develop an inner censor.' It is the inner censor which is the enemy.

This same attitude was expressed at a higher level during another conversation I had with one of the well-known Soviet writers some months before the Twentieth Congress. He had been telling me about his experiences during the thirties. Because he had refused to inform on some of his colleagues he had suffered two years of what amounted to social ostracism. He was not a communist but he had a deep emotional loyalty to the communist ideals. I asked him if he had written about his experiences, saying that, since Sholokov, there had been many interesting small books produced in Soviet literature, but none describing the great conflict between good and evil which was still being played out in his country. I said I could understand that such books could not be published now, but there would come a time when they would be published. He replied: 'How could I write of that? It was too painful, too difficult to know what was wrong and what was right.' I said that if the people like himself remained silent about this struggle, the literature of his country would be impoverished. He said: 'To write of such suffering, to write of such pain, would need an objectivity proper only to a second-rate writer. A great writer has a warmth of heart which commits him to the deepest pain and suffering of his people. But to step back from that experience far enough to write about it would mean a coldness of heart.' I said that what he was saying amounted to a new theory of art. To which he replied: 'Art can look after itself. Art will always recreate itself in different forms. But there are times when humanity is so pitiful and so exposed that art should be willing to stand aside and wait. Art is arrogant unless it is prepared to stand aside.'

This sums up for me, and where I feel it most deeply and personally, the point where 'committedness' can sell out to expediency. Once you admit that 'art should be willing to stand aside for life,' then the little tracts about progress, the false optimism, the dreadful lifeless products of socialist realism, become inevitable.

People who have been influenced by, or who have lived inside, the communist ethos, will understand the complicated emotions, the difficult loyalties, behind what that Soviet writer said. For me it is depressing that the younger people now have no understanding of it. This is the real gap between people of my age and to choose a point at random, people under thirty. Rejecting 'propaganda', for this is what they believe they are doing, they reject an imaginative understanding of what I am convinced is the basic conflict of our time. The mental climate created by the cold war has produced a generation of young intellectuals who totally reject everything communism stands for; they cut themselves off imaginatively from a third of mankind, and impoverish themselves by doing so.

It is this conflict which I am trying to explore in my series of novels, *Children of Violence*, two volumes of which have appeared. Not one critic has understood what I should have thought would be obvious from the first chapter, where I was at pains to state the theme very clearly: that this is a study of the individual conscience in its relations with the collective. The fact that no critic has seen this does not, of course, surprise me. As long as critics are as 'sensitive', subjective, and uncommitted to anything but their own private sensibilities, there will be no body of criticism worth taking seriously in this country. At the moment our critics remind me of a lot of Victorian ladies making out their library lists: this is a 'nice' book; or it is not a 'nice' book; the characters are 'nice'; or they are not 'nice'.

What we need more than anything else, I am convinced, is some serious criticism. The most exciting periods of literature have always been those when the critics were great.

We are not living in an exciting literary period but in a dull one. We are not producing masterpieces, but large numbers of small, quite lively, intelligent novels. Above all, current British literature is provincial. This in spite of the emergence of the Angry Young Men. I use the phrase, not because I think it is in any way an adequate description, but because it is immediately recognizable.

When as a socialist I look forward to the working class being emancipated into readers and writers of serious literature, it is not because I believe books 'about' workers are better than books by or about middle-class people. I make a point of saying this because it is assumed that this is what socialists believe. It is because when a hitherto inarticulate class is released into speech, it brings a fresh rush of vitality into literature. This is why the work of the angry young men was like an injection of vitality into the withered arm of British literature. It expresses something new; a section of the intelligentsia who are scornful of middle-class values; reject 'The Establishment'; are refreshingly derisive and are not prepared to be bullied by phrases like 'good taste'. Yet they are extremely provincial and I do not mean by provincial that they come from or write about the provinces. I mean that their horizons are bounded by their immediate experience of British life and standards.

As an example there is John Braine's book, *Room at the Top*, which was compared with Stendhal's work. This comparison exactly pinpoints what I mean. Stendhal's bitterly opportunist heroes sought their various destinies in the painful twilight of the reaction that followed the French Revolution. The grandeur of Stendhal's vision comes precisely from his bitter knowledge of the pettiness of life after a great vision had failed. But the hero of *Room at the Top*, whose values are similar to Stendhal's heroes, who understand, as clearly as Julien Sorel when he is allowing himself to be corrupted, does not see himself in relation to any larger vision. Therefore he remains petty.

It seems to me that the work of all the new younger writers is essentially a protest against the pettiness and narrowness of what is offered them. From Jimmy Porter to Lucky Jim they are saying : ' I am too good for what I am offered.' And so they are.

British life is at the moment petty and frustrating. The people in these islands are kindly, pleasant, tolerant; apparently content to sink into ever-greater depths of genteel poverty because of the insistence of our rulers on spending so much of the wealth we produce on preparations for a war against communism; a war which will take place if and when the United States decides. They are a people who have lost the habit of fighting back; they will emigrate, but they won't rebel, or at least, not about fundamentals. If there is industrial strife, even socialist newspapers behave like anxious maiden aunts, exhorting both sides to play the game and not to step outside the rules of fair play. For the workers are striking because their standard of living is fluctuating, not because a fifth of the products of their work is being spent on armaments which almost at once become obsolete; not because this is a rich country being artificially kept poor. If there is a disciplinary war against a dissident colony, the young men obediently march off, because they have been educated not to think, or because war experience is likely to be the only exciting and interesting experience they can look forward to. The working people get their view of life through a screen of high-pressure advertising;

sex-sodden newspapers and debased films and television; the middle classes, from a press which from *The Times* to the *New Statesman* is debilitated by a habit of languid conformity which is attacking Britain like dry rot.

It is a country so profoundly parochial that people like myself, coming in from outside, never cease to marvel. Do the British people know that all over what is politely referred to as the Commonwealth, millions of people continually discuss and speculate about their probable reactions to this or that event? No, and if they did, they would not care. I remember being in the House of Commons one afternoon when some Colonial issue was being discussed. There were more Africans in the Strangers' Gallery than there were Members of Parliament who thought the matter important enough to take their seats in the House. Does the Labour movement understand that hundreds of thousands of the more intelligent people in the Colonies, people whose awakening has very often been fed by the generous age of British literature— poets like Shelley and Byron and Burns, writers like Dickens— look to them for help and guidance? For the most part, socialists are not very interested in what is going on in the Colonies. To discuss politics in Britain with most people means that in five minutes one is astounded to find that the talk is of whether old Freddie or Tony is going to be sent out to govern New South Wales, or whether brother John or Jack will be the next secretary of the Trade Union.

Thinking internationally means choosing a particular shade of half-envious, half-patronizing emotion to feel about the United States; or collecting money for Hungary, or taking little holidays in Europe, or liking French or Italian films.

Meanwhile the world churns, bubbles and ferments.

All over that enormous land-mass, the Soviet Union and China, the most epic movement of change ever known in history is taking place. It is the greatest event of our time, and one in which we are all involved. But, to quote a young intellectual aged about twenty-five: ' All that sort of thing, my dear, is really rather *vieux jeu*, isn't it? I mean to say, progress and all that is rather old hat.'

And the most exciting and interesting writers we are producing in this country, for all their vitality, are sunk inside the parochialism.

Mr Amis, for instance, who says he envies writers who have a cause to inspire them: Colonial freedom, for instance. This is the Victorian charitable view; the poor are always with us, suitable objects for uplifting emotions. For apparently Mr Amis, although a Welshman, does not see Britain in intimate relation and interaction with other countries. Mr Amis also says that self-interest is the only authentic political motive. Without going into the psychological analysis of motives, which always cuts too many ways to be useful, the fact is that everywhere in the world people with nothing to gain from being socialists (nothing to gain in the sense that Mr Amis uses) have become, are becoming, and will become, socialists of one kind or another. Most of the people I have known during the past fifteen years have devoted themselves to causes against their self-interest. Britain has been supremely a country which fed people into various crusading movements, either at home or abroad, people with nothing to gain but the maintenance of their self-respect. Mr Amis is generalizing from an emotion which is current among a section of his generation now. It is a temporary mood of disillusion.

There is Mr Colin Wilson, who sees no reason why he should not state that: 'Like all my generation I am anti-humanist and anti-materialist.' Mr Wilson has every right to be anti-humanist and anti-materialist; but it is a sign of his invincible British provincialism that he should claim to speak for his generation. The fact is that outside the very small sub-class of humanity Mr Wilson belongs to, vast numbers of young people are both humanist and materialist. Millions of young people in China, the Soviet Union, and India for instance. And the passions that excite the young African nationalist, five years literate, watching the progress of dams building in India and China, because he knows that what goes on in other countries intimately affects himself, have little in common with the passions of Mr Wilson. Mr Wilson may find the desire of backward people not to starve, not to remain illiterate, rather uninteresting but he and people like him should at least try and understand it exists, and what a great and creative force it is, one which will affect us all.

Then there is Mr Osborne, whose work, if I understand it rightly, is a passionate protest against littleness. There are no great causes left to fight for. Jimmy Porter is doomed to futility because he was born too late for the French Revolution. Admittedly Stendhal exclaimed: ' Happy the heroes who died before 1804,' but that was quite a long time ago. But because other people have done the fighting for Jimmy Porter in the thirties and the forties, there is nothing for it but to stagnate and submit to being sucked dry by women. I think I quote more or less correctly.

But when it reaches the point where we are offered the sex war as a serious substitute for social struggle, even if ironically, then it is time to examine the reasons. That there are no pure causes left? True; but occasions as simply and obviously just as the Storming of the Bastille don't often occur in history. And in the thirties a good deal of passion went into causes complicated by the split in the socialist movement; and in the forties people were prepared to die in order to defend the bad against the worse.

The other day I met a girl who said she envied me because I had had at least ten years of being able to believe in the purity of communism; which advantage was denied to her generation. All of us, she said, were living off the accumulated fat of the socialist hump. She was a socialist herself, but without any enthusiasm.

But what is this socialist hump it seems that we, the middle-aged, are living off? Somebody once said that there was nothing more arrogant than to demand a perfect cause to identify oneself with. It is true that when I became a communist, emotionally if not organizationally, in 1942, my picture of socialism as developed in the Soviet Union was, to say the least, inaccurate. But after fifteen years of uncomfortable adjustment to reality I still find myself in the possession of an optimism about the future obviously considered jejune by anyone under the age of thirty. (In Britain, that is.) Perhaps it is that the result of having been a communist is to be a humanist.

For a while I imagined that the key to this disillusionment might be found by comparing our time with the disillusionment which followed the French Revolution. To this end I re-read Stendhal. ' Injustice and absurdity still made him angry in spite of himself, and he was still angrier at being so, and at taking an interest in that absurd and rascally mob which forms the immense majority of mankind.' 'It is the party spirit,' replied Altamira. 'There are no longer any genuine passions in the nineteenth century; that is why people are so bored in France. We commit the greatest cruelties, but without cruelty.' Such remarks seem contemporary enough.

Yet we are all of us, directly or indirectly, caught up in a great whirlwind of change; and I believe that if an artist has once felt this, in himself, and felt himself as part of it; if he has once made the effort of imagination necessary to comprehend it, it is an end of despair, and the aridity of self-pity. It is the beginning of something else which I think is the minimum act of humility for a writer: to know that one is a writer at all because one represents, makes articulate, is continuously and invisibly fed by, numbers of people who are inarticulate, to whom one belongs, to whom one is responsible.

Because this is not a great age of literature it is easy to fall into despondency and frustration. For a time I was depressed because I thought it likely that the novel might very well be on the way out altogether. It was, after all, born with the middle class, and might die with the middle class. A hundred years ago people used to wait impatiently for the next instalment of a novel. Cinema and television have been added to the popular arts, where once the novel was alone.

But the novelist has one advantage denied to any of the other artists. The novel is the only popular art-form left where the artist speaks directly, in clear words, to his audience. Film-makers, playwrights, television writers, have to reach people through a barrier of financiers, actors, producers, directors. The novelist talks, as an individual to individuals, in a small personal voice. In an age of committee art, public art, people may begin to feel again a need for the small personal voice; and this will feed confidence into writers and, with confidence because of the knowledge of being needed, the warmth and humanity and love of people which is essential for a great age of literature.

Beyond
the Outsider

COLIN WILSON

Colin Wilson

Born in Leicester, 1931. Father in boot and shoe trade. Won a scholarship to Gateway Secondary Technical School. Wrote first book at thirteen, six volumes attempting to summarize the world's scientific knowledge, including psychology and philosophy. While working as a lab. assistant, became deeply interested in literature and renounced science to take up writing plays, short stories, essays and poetry. Entered Civil Service at seventeen and became established in Tax Office. 1949: went into R.A.F. but only for six months. Wandered about England doing navvying jobs. 1950: in Paris, met Raymond Duncan, brother of Isadora, the dancer. Was greatly influenced by Duncan's philosophy of actionalism. A job as hospital porter in Fulham, then again in Paris working on *Merlin* and *Paris Review*. 1954: back in England, slept on Hampstead Heath for six months to save rent, writing a novel during the day in the British Museum reading room. Angus Wilson, then assistant superintendent of the reading room, offered to read manuscript and Wilson began a critical book, *The Outsider*. Wrote this while working in Espresso bars. Publication of *The Outsider* (1956) enabled him to give his full time to writing a sequel, *Religion and the Rebel*.

WHEN it was first suggested to me, the idea of writing a credo seemed unreasonable. I have now spent about a quarter of a million words outlining what I believe—in my critical books *The Outsider* and *Religion and the Rebel*—and a credo could only attempt to condense these two books. Closer reflection made me realize that there is an alternative: to state 'what I believe' in far more frankly personal terms than is possible in a critical book. This is what I intend to do in the following pages.

My mind, unfortunately, is not systematic or academic. My vision of the world is completely 'personal', and I find it impossible to get far enough away from this subjective bias to write work that could be called 'criticism' or 'speculative philosophy'. My attitude towards writing begins with an obsession; I happen to be obsessed by certain ideas and I think and care about nothing else. These obsessions rise out of certain needs within myself. For a long time, I felt that this state of obsession formed a barrier between myself and the age in which I live. Now I am less certain. Once, I had an intense suspicion of the word *Zeitgeist*, because I did not see how the 'age' could have a spirit. Yet Scott Fitzgerald wrote of his own period: it bore him up, flattered him, and gave him more money than he had dreamed of, simply for telling people that he felt as they did. The same thing seems to be happening to a number of young writers of today—myself among them—so perhaps, after all, there is such a thing as a 'spirit of the age'. So I have come to accept that 'the age' might possibly feel the same needs I feel myself, and have dismissed the fear that I may be seeing only a distorted reflection of my own face. This is my sole reason for writing a 'credo'.

My critical books are essentially *my* vision of the world: just that and no more. For me, they are a groundplan for future creative work; a sort of cellar from which I may go on drawing materials. I state this because there has been some tendency to accuse me of lacking academic precision, of not writing a volume as objective as Mario Praz's *Romantic Agony*. I repeat, therefore: my vision of the world is frankly subjective: as subjective as Blake's in *Vala*. If it has any sort of validity for our time (and I do not assert that it has), it is only because it is in some way typical of this age; not because it was supposed to be an academic examination of the problems of our age.

(This is what I meant to say when, at a 'literary lunch', I explained that *The Outsider* was a fraud: that it was 'dished up' to look like an impersonal appraisal of our time, when in reality it expressed a completely personal vision. In writing it, I was aware of this double-pull; to write a critical analysis of present trends, like Edmund Wilson's *Axel's Castle* (which had been my constant reading for many years); and the desire to get on my soap box (as I had during the summer and autumn of 1953 at Hyde Park) and talk about the way I see things. I had broken off the writing of a novel to write *The Outsider*. For years—since I was sixteen—I had kept a journal, running to many volumes, in which my literary opinions were interspersed with notes for stories, observations, etc. *The Outsider* was only a filtering-off of these journals. Yeats talked of being obsessed by certain symbols, which recurred in his poetry. I am too; and I spoke of them in *The Outsider*; it is essentially a product of obsession. All this I explained in my speech.

I was surprised to find what a sensation these views caused when they were reported in the popular press. A daily newspaper ran a headline: WILSON ADMITS HE IS A FRAUD, and the story was taken up by newspapers in America and on the Continent. I was forced to write several dozen letters to the various papers, explaining that I had not meant that I had written *The Outsider* as a hoax. The denial seemed to cause some disappointment, and most of the newspapers suppressed it as having no news value.

The whole episode revealed to me that the writer in our age is confronted with a quite unique problem; it is no longer simply a question of making himself heard; but of making sure that he is not heard too well.)

32   *   *   *

Our age is essentially unheroic. Heroism is individualism. We live in an age of numbers and labels; workers clock-in and clock-out, and discuss the football results or last night's television programmes. At the same time, it is not an age of oppression and general poverty. The improvement in social conditions has brought about an increase of leisure, which is a freeing of vital energy. Our leisure has underlined once again the problems of meaning and purpose : and has underlined it, not only for the socially privileged (as in Ancient Greece or the Middle Ages) but for the average worker, the mere 'social unit'. The basic human craving for a sense of purpose reasserts itself as a desire to re-create the heroic : to re-create it indiscriminately in the heroes of Everest and Kon-Tiki, in the film star or popular crooner, the 'rebel without a cause' (in its original meaning, the juvenile criminal). My 'Outsider' fitted neatly into the pattern of obsession; consequently, like Scott Fitzgerald, I have found the age 'bearing me up and flattering me' for providing it with a catchword, a symbol, such as James Dean has provided in the fifties, or Rudolph Valentino in the twenties. I have no basic objection to this : for I have also believed that the Outsider is the heroic figure of our time.

*　　　*　　　*

For my own part—as I have explained elsewhere—my own awareness of 'Outsider problems' developed from lack of leisure in my teens, at a time when I needed leisure most. My problem became simply the problem of how to find leisure to read and think and write, when my circumstances made it necessary to work forty-eight hours a week to live. Having found some degree of leisure through the success of my first book, I can hardly now consider myself an 'Outsider' in that sense. In fact, it has been several years since I thought of myself as 'an Outsider' in any sense at all. A man is an Outsider when his life is made wretched by a yearning for freedom—freedom from internal or external problems. But an obvious question arises here : are there not a thousand different types of Outsider—depending on what they want their freedom for?

The trouble with my 'Outsider' category soon came home to me when I thought of writing a book about the Outsider (I was 19 then). I began with Nijinsky, Van Gogh, Lawrence, and projected a chapter on Goethe's *Faust*, and Schiller's *Robbers*, and another on *Oblomov*, *Hamlet* and *The Great Gatsby*—studies in romanticism and hesitation, and further chapters on Nietzsche, Schopenhauer, Boehme and Swedenborg. So far, so good. But now the problem began to widen. I wanted to pursue two directions at once: one into the mystics of the thirteenth and the fourteenth centuries—Eckhart, Tauler, Suso, Catherine of Siena, Gertrude of Helfta—the other, into the great mathematicians and philosophers, with particular reference to George Boole, the inventor of symbolic logic, and his English descendants, Russell and Whitehead, the former of whom I detested. I was not sure what I meant by the contrast, but I was sure that, without mystical premises, philosophy becomes mere logic. (I am only now—having read Wittgenstein—beginning to understand what I meant.) But my point is this: although this discussion of mysticism and science followed naturally from my premises, my term 'Outsider' no longer fitted in anywhere. Obviously, it was useful to *begin* a discussion with, but after a very short time, its usefulness disappeared.

But I had never thought of myself as a philosopher, and soon gave up the idea of the critical book in the interest of writing a novel. (The idea revived three years later when I had temporarily abandoned the novel.) It was not until I read Kierkegaard at the age of 21 that I realized that Kierkegaard had called my 'Outsider-philosophy' Existentialism. Existentialism is the opposite of 'abstract philosophy'. Existentialism is philosophy that begins with the idea of will and imagination, just as 'speculative philosophy' begins with intellect and logic.

Imagination—that was the key-word in my structure, as in Blake's. In my teens, I had experienced moments when the time between events in the past and the present seemed to be completely annihilated; then my imagination seemed to gain a curious power of freeing me from present reality. In those moments humanity appeared to me as a fly that has been scooped out of a cup of cold tea and drags itself over the surface of the table, leaving a wet trail from its wings. Humanity seemed to be tied to present reality, unable to escape from its pressure, except by sleep or alcohol. Events are an everlasting pressure, demanding the attention, crippling imagination. The present raises challenges at every moment of the day. Man does his best to combat these challenges—all of the little things that 'go wrong', the problems of eating and feeding and working and human relations. But sometimes the challenges are too much; they demand more energy and courage than he possesses; then he has a nervous breakdown, or relapses to a lower level of life; deliberately killing his sensibility to protect himself. It is like a man who knows he is about to be sick, who combats the nausea for an hour, lying in bed, and then finds it too much for him. In that appalling moment when the being seems to rend apart, all times of gastric health seem to be degrees of sickness, leading to the moment of nausea as inevitably as gravitation draws objects towards the earth. So it is when sanity is strained by unbearable tensions; all sanity seems to be dubious and slight in the face of the abyss of chaos that means insanity. But there is more reason for regarding this vision as objectively true. Chaos is universal. The average man ropes himself off from the edge of the chaos, and tries to pretend that his tiny area of light and order is the whole universe. He pretends that certainty lies on the other side of his rope-boundary. But man can never know certainty— not unless he becomes God. For the Outsider, the Insider is an ostrich that buries its head in the sand, a self-deceiver.[1]

I must emphasize this view of the 'Insider', for it is of primary importance in my scheme.

There is chaos. The Outsider faces it and attempts to base his

---

[1] When I was fourteen, I saw a picture that was supposed to represent Freud's concept of the unconscious. It was divided into two halves. In one half, a little, bowler-hatted man carries an office briefcase along the pavement of a big city. Other people hurry around him on their way to work. But in the foreground of the picture, just below the edge of the pavement, flat faces thrust themselves up; hairy hands reach for the kerbstones to clamber up. In the second picture—representing the little man's dreams—the hairy sub-men have climbed on to the pavement; they are assaulting the cowering shop-girls and office clerks; and the little man shrinks into a doorway, holding up his briefcase to defend his head.

The first picture—the ape-men below the edge of the pavement —stuck in my mind as a symbol of the Insider's world insulated to the edge of the abyss. But beyond the edge of the pavement lies chaos and terror.

life on its recognition. The Insider deliberately pushes it into his subconscious mind, and fills his consciousness with a selected 'order'. He is afraid of the chaos. And if it were true that the chaos has the last word, he would be right to be afraid of it, to base his life on a refusal to recognize it. Recognition would mean annihilation—or at least, lowered efficiency. (This is why the maturing artist is usually an inefficient, floundering being in the world of the bourgeois.) But the careers of the Beethovens, the Van Goghs, the Dostoevskys, give the lie to this low-spirited view. They affirm that man can be greater than he realizes by launching himself into the sea of chaos. They affirm that by turning his back on 'worldly values', by summoning an apparently suicidal courage, man can achieve a new plane of the heroic, a further step towards the god-like. This is the lesson of the Outsiders—a lesson of deliberate loneliness and reaction against the values of the mass, a revolt against the mob-conditioned desire for security.

Naturally, this revolt is not the last word. If it were, it would be no more than the romantic revolt of Schiller's *Robbers*, where Karl Moor praises anarchy but longs secretly for order—a superhuman order maintained by god-like men. No, beyond the Outsider's contempt of security lies the simple business-man's principle: nothing ventured, nothing gained. The Outsider's suicidal courage creates a world of value so much higher than the world we have made for ourselves that it seems supernatural, the world of Beethoven's last quartets, of Mozart's *Zauberflöte*, of *The Brothers Karamazov*, or the last act of *Back to Methuselah*.

The romantic ring of this is deceptive. All real romanticism is the beginning of classicism (as it was with Goethe). All real humanism is the beginning of a new religious attitude. 'If the fool would persist in his folly, he would become wise.' Romanticism is only distinguished from realism by its character of velleity. If a shopgirl dreams of marrying a millionaire, she is a romantic. But if she deliberately sets out to catch a millionaire and succeeds, she is no longer a romantic but a realist. The child with a longing for the moon is a romantic, like the child who longs to see ancient Troy. But the child who grows up with an interest in space travel has become a realist, like Heinrich Schliemann, who went out and dug up ancient Troy because of a childhood dream. The Outsider with a longing for the infinite, for perfection, is a romantic. But the Outsider who sets out to find a discipline to discover infinity, perfection, is a realist.

My reason for rejecting the label 'romantic' for myself can be expressed in a few sentences. I believe that our civilization is in decline, and that Outsiders are a symptom of that decline. They are men in reaction against scientific materialism; *men who would once have found their orientation in the Church.* I believe that when a civilization begins to produce Outsiders, it has received a challenge: a challenge to produce a higher type of man, and give itself a new unity of purpose, or to slip into the gulf after all the other civilizations that have failed to respond to the challenge. The 'Outsider' is the individual who attempts to respond to the challenge.

I have stated my belief flatly, and I do not intend to adduce evidence in its support at this point. For the evidence, I can only recommend the reader who has not already done so to study *The Decline of the West* and Arnold Toynbee's *A Study of History*. In the course of this essay I will attempt to explain my belief more fully.

*   *   *

The Outsider needs an escape from himself. The case of T. E. Lawrence made this clear. Tolstoy's madman says: 'I am running away from something dreadful and cannot escape it. I am always with myself, and it is I who am my tormentor. . . . Neither the Penza nor any other property will add anything or take anything from me; it is myself I am weary of, and find intolerable and a torment. I want to fall asleep and forget myself, and cannot. I cannot get away from myself.' Lawrence said: 'I did not like the "myself" I could see and hear.' The Outsider's personality is a prison and a torment.

One would be justified in saying: But *millions* of people feel like that. Tired housewives or business men say: 'I am going to the cinema to *get away from myself* for a bit,' and we hear it said of a good book or film: 'It takes you out of yourself.' And this is perfectly true. The human personality is like a room. To a large extent, we build this room ourselves; but circumstances, environment, help to make it too. We also furnish the room: with human beings—or rather, their images—familiar places and actions. When you have lived in the same room for years, it becomes all you know: 'Five windows light the caverned man; through one he breathes the air. . . .'

Every deep emotional or intellectual experience is an enlarging of the room; has a ripening effect, a maturing effect on the personality. This is a commonplace.

But new experiences cannot reach us while we are still in the room. That is why people want to 'forget themselves'. Without self-forgetfulness, there is no development; men and women would remain crabbed and undeveloped; their energies would stagnate.

Most of us manage to adjust ourselves to our 'rooms'. We get used to them. By the time we die at 75 or so, we have accepted the room. We think it is us. We identify ourselves with it completely.

The young man of genius—the young Shelley or Rimbaud or Fitzgerald—is still busy drawing up plans for building his room. He is determined it will be vast—so vast that he will never get tired of being in it. He is determined to furnish it with all kinds of intellectual and emotional recreations, so that he can never be bored. Usually, he is determined not to get tied up with any single person —a wife or lover—because he reserves the right to change the furniture completely every now and then. His room is, in fact, a huge blueprint, full of possibilities. Above all else, the man of genius wants to be the supreme architect of his personality. And he realizes that, if he is to continue to grow and mature as he gets older (and not simply stagnate, as most people do) he must never allow the desire for comfort and warmth to overcome the urge to make himself grow spiritually. This desire constitutes his integrity.

The Outsider is a man whose instinct is towards spiritual growth, but who has allowed his room to encase him tightly. He does not understand what is troubling him. He doesn't even know he is in a room—he thinks he lives 'in the world', like all other human beings. *He identifies himself with the room.* He begins to hate himself—that is, hate the room. Everything he sees, he sees through its grimy windows. He breathes its bad air. No experience reaches him in his room—or if it does it reaches him so filtered and diluted that it does no good.

Gurdjieff pointed out that no human being can live without a continual 'food' of experience, impressions. We can live for weeks without food and water. We can live for minutes without air. But we would die if our food of impressions were cut off, even for a second. If this is true, it follows that to live on diluted experience which has been filtered through the dirty windows and thick walls of the personality is as bad as drinking malarial water or eating food out of dustbins. Its effect is a spiritual indigestion.

The spiritual health of the individual—and therefore of the community—can only be guaranteed by making sure that he can escape from his room periodically—or at least open the doors and windows, and let some air and sunlight in.

Using this analogy, the problems of the Outsider become clearer. While the Outsider—the George Fox or Ramakrishna or Dosto-evsky—was shut up in his personality, he was miserable. When his spiritual agony had given him enough strength to dare to smash one of the windows, he became a healthy man again.

Nevertheless the room we live in is not a prison. It can *become* a prison, and often does. But it is there to protect us. None of us could bear an everlasting bombardment of experience; it would drive us insane in twenty-four hours. So we want a room into which we can lock ourselves tightly, and barricade the windows and bar the doors. Then experience pounds harmlessly outside, like volleys of wind, and we can sleep. Too much experience is spiritual death. Rimbaud and Gauguin illustrate this.

The complexity of modern experience has driven us all—quite imperceptibly—to strengthen our personalities—to get extra shut-ters for the windows and bars for the doors. We have perfected a gadget for cutting all noises from the outside world—nobody wants to hear the everlasting clatter and clamour of a modern city all the time. And our room becomes more like a fortress every day. A fortress is a prison.

Our modern civilization is doing this to us. Its complexity defeats us. When T. S. Eliot gave up editing *The Criterion* in 1939, he confessed that it was because the times had 'induced in myself a depression of spirits so different from any other experience of fifty years as to be a new emotion'; and it was Eliot who had earlier used the phrase 'the gigantic canvas of anarchy and chaos that is our age'. And yet if the artist cannot remain serene and unaffected by his age—in his work at least—who can?

I have tried to show that the Outsider is a man with an unusual and acute need for a sense of values. It has been objected that almost everybody asks himself at some time: What is life all about? and that therefore everybody is, in some degree, an Outsider. But this is only a failure to understand the spiritual condition of a man who feels a perpetual gnawing instinct for meaning, a hunger and thirst: a thirst that can be so acute that its frustration can lead to insanity. When a man is more or less contented, his mind occupied with business matters or the football pools, he likes to think that he is not forgetting anything terribly important, or leaving any vital element out of account. If you were to remind him of the existence of Beethoven quartets, he might say: Yes, but there's a time and place for everything. He would like to believe that what you think important is a relative matter; that it is quite right that one moment you should feel that dinner is important, another, that business is important, and still another, that music or art or the theatre is important. This sort of relativity comes quite naturally to us all; it doesn't strike us as inconsistency. But the Outsider has a feeling that there are certain things that are absolutely important, and that, quite literally, should occupy the mind all the time, and be a perpetual standard of reference for all other feelings.

The only other man who shares this belief with him is the religious man. Religion makes precisely the same demands for meaning and purpose as the Outsider. The Outsider is therefore akin to the religious man.

Now there can be no doubt whatever that, in previous centuries, it has been religion that has supplied the ordinary man with his sense of meaning and purpose: that has assured him that the world is not a 'devil-ridden chaos' or a 'gigantic canvas of anarchy'. Two centuries of free-thinking have smashed Christianity. I do not pretend that it is not still widely believed and accepted. But it is no more generally accepted nowadays than the Greek gods were in the time of Socrates, or the Roman gods in the time of Marcus Aurelius. The time when it served as a cement to hold Western civilization together is over, and there is no point in not facing this fact.

The civilization is like the Outsider. It must have a religion to survive. We have seen enough of 'humanism' and scientific 'progress' to know how much they are worth; they engender nothing but mass-boredom and frustration, and periodic outbreaks of world-war. Only the professors and professional philosophers fail to see this; they are never less than a century out of date.

I have tried to show how the Outsider can fight his way back from the sense of meaninglessness and futility to a religion. By a purely existential analysis—I mean an analysis that refuses to theorize or accept anything on faith—he arrives at some sort of recognition of the human position: a recognition that man is born bent and twisted, is a smashed radio set. The deepest, clearest perception of the reality of the world is the perception of complete terror. The visionary's moments of insight prove to him that man is not a fraction of what he could be; that he has never explored a fragment of his potential greatness, which is not the preposterous fairy tale of man's scientific greatness, but a possibility of a certainty of purpose, an intensity of spiritual discipline, that is almost inconceivable in our soiled and bewildered era.

From his insight into the human position, his 'glimpse into chaos', the Outsider acquires a sense of purpose and will. He instantly ceases to be an Outsider and becomes a spiritual reformer. He may embrace an orthodox religion—like Ramakrishna or Fox—but he is driven by something deeper than Hinduism or Christianity: by an urge to serve a power he now recognizes inside him, an evolutionary force of whose purpose he has become aware. This conviction sweeps away the frustration and incertitude that make an Outsider.

And what of the civilization? What happens when the whole civilization begins to suffer from Outsider's disease? The men who clock in and clock out every day, the women who travel to work by the same bus every morning, the youths in the warehouses and civil service offices—what happens when they begin to hate the civilization that treats them like cog-wheels? The Outsider makes a lonely spiritual effort, and feels the sense of purpose mount in

him. These uncomprehending half-rebels never understand themselves enough to put up a real fight. They haven't the stuff of
spiritual reformers in them.

But they flock to the films and football matches, or to hear the
latest crooner or evangelist at Harringay; any stupidity is better
than their meaningless world. Whatever meaning their world has
is given to it by financiers and film stars, crooks and charlatans.

In a past age, it was the men of genius who gave the world its
meaning. Their laws made the Church; their ideas, their art, their
practical sense, were present everywhere. As civilization declines,
the man of genius becomes the hole-in-corner man. His ideas
cease to reach the common man; his art is incomprehensible to
the worker. He stands back, and the advertising king takes his
place; when the common man picks up a magazine, or switches
on a radio, or goes to a cinema, he gets a distorted, cheapened
version of what he is *supposed* to like.

But instinctively, the world is still on the side of the man of
genius. When tastes get too debased, there is a reaction, a revul-
sion. Instinctively, all healthy life demands that standards be
raised, not lowered, as a healthy army prefers discipline to laziness
and inanimation. In all men there is an intuitive recognition that
increased discipline means increased vitality: that, as Socrates
expressed it, the undisciplined life is not worth living. That is why,
when the religion of a country ceases to provide a discipline, we
glorify the army and the government.

The Outsider's sickness is an instinctive craving for discipline.
He is too intelligent to serve a cause that his intellect finds contemptible. Consequently, he must find a discipline that his critical
intellect can approve—a moral discipline, a spiritual discipline.

But society lacks the Outsider's penetrating critical intellect. In
its secret craving for a discipline, for something to follow, it runs
after every fire-eating politician, every heart-throb evangelist,
every dictator with a programme.

This is what happens when the Outsiders cease to be the spiritual
leaders of the society.

There is the problem in a nutshell. The superficiality of our
leaders brings us nearer every year to the inevitable end. The
cheapness of our ideas, the mere surface-philosophy that lies be-

hind our mass-production drives, the dreariness of the materialism that underlies our concept of progress, the pseudo-philosophy of our professors—such men as Ayer and Russell—take us closer to the complete breakdown of our civilization day by day.

I do not know whether there is a way out. I can only try to indicate what conditions would have to be fulfilled if our civilization were to be saved. The Outsider is the key. But our civilization is old, and maybe a key is not enough.

If the Outsider ceased to be an Outsider, and became a spiritual driving-force in society, he would need an organization to support him. In the past, that organization was the religion of the country. From the Buddha, five centuries before Christ, to Sri Ramakrishna nineteen centuries after, it is obvious that the Outsider is only at home in a religious framework. That framework is ceasing to exist in the world today; one by one, religions are discarded, and political ideologies take their place. Tibet is now run on Marxian lines.

We must remake it or perish. I am not optimistic. But the problem is worth examining.

* * *

In the introduction to his *Experiment in Autobiography*, H. G. Wells has a passage that strikes me as being of peculiar importance; I cannot quote it in full, but here is its essence:

' Most individual creatures, since life began, have been " up against it " all the time, have been driven continually by fear and cravings, have had to respond to the unresting antagonisms of their surroundings, and they have found a sufficient and sustaining interest in the drama of immediate events provided for them by these demands. Essentially, their living was continual adjustment to happenings. [*Vide* Sartre in *La Nausée*, speaking of the café proprietor : " When his café empties, his head empties too."] Good hap and ill hap filled it entirely. They hungered and ate, and they desired and loved . . . and they died.

But with the dawn of human foresight, and with the appearance of a great surplus of energy in life such as the last century or so has revealed, there has been a progressive emancipation of the attention from everyday urgencies. What was once the whole of life, has become to an increasing extent, merely a background of life. People can ask now what would have been an extraordinary question five hundred years ago. They can say: " Yes, you earn a living, you support a family, you love and hate, but—*what do you do?*"

Conceptions of living, divorced more and more from immediacy, distinguish the modern civilized man from all former life . . . We are like early amphibians, so to speak, struggling out of the waters that have hitherto covered our kind, into the air, seeking to breathe in a new fashion. . . . '

This last sentence recalls Marcel Proust, with his cork-lined room off the Boulevard Haussmann; his retreat into it divided his primary from his secondary life. The primary life is that simple life of the body and of events. Once upon a time, it would have been enough to call it just ' living ', for it was the only life that creatures on this planet had ever known. But now the life of the mind becomes increasingly important, and it brings with it the question of meaning and purpose. It brings self-reflection. The question of meaning does not appear until the secondary life begins to assume an importance close to that of the primary life, or exceeding it. *Meaning is a concept of that secondary life.*

*   *   *

The masterpieces of the ' centuries of faith ' were all pivoted on the *Weltanschauung* of the Church: the *Divina Commedia*, the *Canterbury Tales*, *Orlando Furioso*, *The Faerie Queene*. In later ages, romanticism or agnosticism served the same purpose, and gave coherence to *The Revolt of Islam*, *Don Carlos*, *In Memoriam*, *Tess of the D'Urbervilles*. Great ages of literature have a common basis of faith. This is what is lacking in our own age. Our art has no common pivot. Having lost the original die, the artists can only imitate one another's patterns. Schools of imitators follow any successful writer or painter; not because the imitators themselves lack talent, but because they lack a tradition into which to channel their talent; one successful innovator constitutes a ' tradition '.

For thirty years now, this talk of tradition has been a commonplace of literary criticism—especially in American universities, where the influence of Eliot and Pound is stronger than in England. But for twenty years, it has been obvious what 'tradition' means in practice for these two eminent men of letters: for Eliot, Anglicanism; for Pound, a humanistic Confucianism.

My own attitude towards these 'commitments' is by no means critical; I feel that it is a very fine thing—if you can do it. I do not, like many modern critics, feel that there was 'intellectual treason' in Mr Eliot's act of accepting the dogmas of a church; it required a determination and courage—and above all, a capacity for *hard work*—that most of its critics do not possess. But this can hardly be regarded as a solution that is valid for all our civilization. If it required all Mr Eliot's fine intelligence and a sort of higher mathematics of faith to make him into a practising Christian, there seems little enough hope even for his less gifted contemporaries, let alone for the anonymous millions who make up a civilization.

And at this point, the issues become very clear. A religious faith is plainly the mortar that binds the bricks of civilization together; without it, the civilization begins to produce discontented Outsiders like pimples, and suffers from a general deterioration of health. A motive is necessary, a common aim; and the need becomes an element in the general condition, the 'intellectual climate' of the civilization.

What are the conditions that produce new religions? And are they available in our civilization today?

The first and most obvious can be stated immediately. All the great religions were founded by one man, a law-giver: Mahomet, Moses, Zoroaster, Christ, Gautama. That is most important.

But then, as T. E. Lawrence pointed out, such men are not unusual. 'The Arabs said there had been forty thousand prophets.' It is doubtful whether it is only the personal quality of the prophet that makes him the founder of a religion; one might guess that Mahomet's personal character was not as forceful or as integrated as Elijah's, yet he had a great deal more influence on history. No, it is plain that the conditions are almost as important as the man. In the political field examples like Hitler and Mussolini show that social unrest, and a feeling of disillusionment and approaching crisis, give the reformer his opportunity to become dictator. More-

B*

over, new religions usually spring out of the old ones when the older creeds are getting senile, as Buddhism grew out of Hinduism, or Christianity out of Judaism. In this one respect, our civilization can certainly be regarded as being ready for a new religion.

But there is an aspect of the problem that I have not spoken of; it is this: religion fastens its grip on the civilization through the *ordinary people*; the people of *primary lives*. A certain climate of credulity is necessary to it. But our civilization has very little of this primary level credulity left. Incredulity is the inheritance of our century; religious unbelief is general. For the ordinary man, religion means believing a lot of nonsensical statements about vicarious atonement, the holy trinity, the virgin birth, etc.

My aim in writing *The Outsider* was to demonstrate that a religious position can be arrived at by continuous doubting and unending questioning—by a completely sceptical approach. Its content could be summarized: Provided you feel an acute need for some solid belief, and are prepared to look far enough, you can arrive at a religious position in which there are no elements of superstition. Admittedly, to do so requires a peculiar persistence—a persistence that springs from a ' hunger and thirst' after faith. This seriousness of temperament—the determination to find a justification for living—is always pretty rare. And this is the centre of the problem. *For the individual's problem, the problem of the Outsider, is now the problem of the whole civilization.* Well, the Outsider has retraced the road from philosophy—from total scepticism—to religion. Can the civilization do it too?

The obvious answer—obvious, yet not necessarily true—is No. In which case we must smash.

The road from religion to philosophy is easy; in the Middle Ages, every scholar travelled it. But the road back—from philosophy to religion—is uphill, and requires an unusual toughness of temperament and persistence to travel it.

Religion *must* be the answer. Humanistic liberalism won't do. And yet this is hardly fully recognized today. Recently a well-known writer of the thirties asked me: ' Why clamour for a religion? We have great poetry, great music, great art to elevate our spirits. *I* don't need a religion.' It was difficult to answer him, for one could see he didn't. It would have been no reply to say:

I do. There are millions in present-day society who think as he does—not because they have 'great art, great music' etc., but because the circumstances of their lives are such that they experience no sense of strain—nothing, anyway, that a pint and a game of darts can't cure. The same went for my friend (for he is a friend, in spite of my dislike of his attitude). Could one talk to him of the increasing complexity of civilization that concentrates on making man a cog in a machine : of the development of Russia towards Orwell's *1984* and of England and America towards Huxley's *Brave New World*? There are millions who are not appalled by this, who point to our technical advance, to the increasing number of working men who spend their holidays on the Continent and have television sets, and ask : What's wrong with our civilization? There is nothing whatever in common between these people and a Jonathan Swift, whose attitude to men was summarized in the words : Perish the day on which I was born!

The belief of the Middle Ages was in original sin and the need for salvation. The belief today is in progress, and the idea that our cleverness brings us nearer every day to the Heaven upon Earth of Reason made perfect. Admittedly, there are exceptions even among leading figures of the age. Sir James Jeans and Sir Arthur Eddington were both religious men; the scientist now tends to admit that *omnia exeunt in mysterium*—all things lead back to the incomprehensible. But then one picks up a newspaper and reads about the exploits of Billy Graham or Dr Frank Buchman, and realizes despairingly that for the educated man of today religion stinks of self-deluding evangelism. Religion means the insane crankery of Jehovah's Witnesses, or some negro messiah shouting 'I got God,' not—as in the Middle Ages—a rigorous intellectual system, based upon the experience and insights of great saints, fortified by the best brains of the age. For a religion to be alive, the life of the time has to flow into it, the most vital currents of the age : the thought of an Aquinas, the painting of a Fra Angelico, the music of a Palestrina. Our age is the victim of a terrible bifurcation. Its art and its philosophy are no longer joined by the same axle.

Hence the Outsider.

* * *

In what sense is the Outsider particularly a twentieth-century figure?

This question carries us beyond the scope of my book *The Outsider*, where I content myself by defining him and his problems. But the answer is obvious and straightforward. Self-expression means the bringing-to-birth of some idea or concept. It means transferring the idea out of the sphere of mere thought into the sphere of action. In primitive people—primary level people—there is no great gap between an idea and the action. Thought and action are hardly ever separated. Even the story-telling and the art depends upon straightforward action, hunting or war. The music is intended to be danced to or marched to.

The time comes when certain men develop secondary powers, and become interested in things that have no immediate relation to action—in numbers, in the stars, in tragedy or comedy for its own sake; and finally, in philosophy.

These men, the artists and philosophers, are not Outsiders. They are held in great respect by the more practical men, who regard them with awe, and expect them to foretell the future from numbers or the stars, or the will of the gods from philosophy. They become priests and rulers and ' sages '. There is always a feeling of direct intercourse between them and the ' practical ' part of the civilization. They do not get the feeling of being useless dreamers. As the religion develops, these men become the spearheads of the civilization, for it is their inventiveness and culture that raises the standard of life; their laws are obeyed by the people.

Inevitably, there is a deterioration. Men inherit the authority who have no sense of purpose. Men who have a sense of purpose are ignored because they were born into the wrong class. The old laws harden into mere observances. The sense of over-all purpose that inspired the original law-givers begins to fail. And this is quite natural. Just as a scientist nowadays must first learn all the work of his predecessors before he can start doing original work, so the new law-givers would need to inherit all the old grasp of the civilization's problems, *and* all the new complexities. More effort of assimilation is needed. And unfortunately—as Elijah pointed out—men are not born better or wiser than their fathers. So all that happens is that new men are irritated into rebelling and overthrowing the old laws and law-givers, and making themselves law-givers in their place. But the new men are usually hard-headed and brash, and lack the depth and mellowness that the tradition conferred on the old law-givers. The result is that the new leaders become even less satisfactory than the old ones.

Naturally, there is a revolt against the laws themselves. The men with intellectual powers are no longer the automatic supporters of the religion and the law; they begin to develop along their own lines. Now the split that creates Outsiders is well on the way. For the intellectual activities of the men of genius are not only separated from the law and religion; they even begin to lose the sanction of law and religion, and the Galileo is forced to swear that the earth does not go round the sun. This is not a permanent setback, for the men of genius always triumph eventually. But when genius and the law have separated, the deterioration begins.

Genius is only a sense of purpose and direction, and the greatest geniuses are the men who can feel intuitively the whole drift of a civilization. The men of genius are naturally the law-givers. But unfortunately, they are unconnected with the religion of the age —except for an occasional Pascal or Newman or Coleridge. They begin to create their own religions. The scientists create a religion of science ('natural religion'); the poets create a religion of inspiration (romanticism). And the stage is well prepared for chaos. For the scientist is now the only man of intellect who can put his intellectual insights into action, and see them influencing the mind of the age: Descartes, Newton, Einstein, Freud, Darwin. The poet and creative artist are now regarded as beings of a very inferior order. Many of them accept their time's low estimate of themselves, and drift into a morose subjectivism, write gloomy and neurotic stories and poems, painting incomprehensible pictures. They are now no longer the intellectual leaders and spearheads of the age; at best, they become fashionable and popular with an artistic 'set'. For the farmer and the aeroplane mechanic, they mean nothing. *There is a gap between thought and action.* The fact of being meaningless to a farmer drives the artist into deeper subjectivism.

Now the scientist is, as often as not, a moral imbecile. The greatest scientists—the Newtons, Galileos, Einsteins—have possessed

49

no deep sense of the moral significance of life. Newton's religiousness took the form of working out a chronology of the Bible, treating the Bible not as inspiration and insight, but as raw material for calculation. Einstein was a humanist whose 'moral sense' was no more than a hatred of all cruelty and bigotry— which, valuable as it may be, is not the first characteristic of a great religious mind.

It is the man with the over-all sense of purpose of life and of man who is the great religious force. In our age, this man is the Outsider. He is morally alive. He asks of life: 'Why?' He asks of his own life: 'To what purpose?' In past ages, this man would have been a father of the Church—or at least, a respected and saintly man. In our age, his sense of 'Why?' has no room to develop—or at least, the odds against which it develops are tremendous.

If he is determined and persistent, and doesn't let the problems permanently crush his spirit, he begins to develop a sense that there is something wrong with our civilization. It is only a vague sense, and may only express itself as 'I don't want to be a cog in a machine' or something of the kind. But the more he faces the problem and attacks it, the greater becomes his appetite for higher vitality, for seizing his deepest purpose and accomplishing it.

Sören Kierkegaard was among the first to devote his life to expressing this anti-civilization point of view. For him, a timid social thinker—although a great moral one—the attack on Western civilization became an attack on its chief product, 'abstract philosophy' (which Blake had also made war on half a century earlier). Abstract philosophy is what happens when thinkers cease to ask questions about the purpose of life and the aim of man, and ask semi-scientific questions, like: 'How do we know that things are really what they appear to be?'

It is not merely 'abstract philosophy' that is guilty. It is the whole of Western civilization. Only 'scientific' modes of thought are acceptable. Insight and vision are unacceptable. But these are the Outsider's stock in trade.

There is a point of such importance here that I must say it with all possible emphasis: the Outsider is NOT anti-rational. It is not Reason he objects to; it is the tiny area of existence that 'rational thinkers' apply their reason to. For the Outsider, this is only a bit of existence—the world of physical fact. Obviously, the world of physical fact is strictly only the bit of space and time that is here-and-now. To make any attempt at thought at all, the scientist has to assume parts of existence that are not here-and-now, and are not, therefore, 'facts'. The scientist is only confined to physical facts that can be measured. The Outsider is concerned with equally real facts—the pain you feel when someone close dies, the pleasure you feel on hearing music—and uses precisely the same method as the scientist; that is to say, he keeps asking: Why? and: How? He is puzzled by the knowledge that if you let yourself be taken in by the human pageant (if I can be forgiven the cliché), you experience an unanswerable sense of: Why are we here? Where are we going? If you live on a level of ordinary human emotions, and let them fill your horizon—as most people do—life is an insoluble puzzle. Any sort of answer depends upon greater and greater detachment from the human race—seeing people spread out in space and time, and not feeling yourself one of them; not being taken in by their viewpoint. The scientist, of course, begins to do this. One of the finest evocations of the place of the human ants in the vast universe is in the beginning of Sir James Jeans's *Mysterious Universe*. But the Outsider soon realizes that the scientist's view of time is far more limited. He knows all about the rocks of the Cretaceous era, but nothing about the real state of mind of the authors of the Upanishads or St Augustine. In these matters, he makes absurd over-simplifications, and talks vaguely about superstition and anthropomorphism. The scientist's knowledge is not wide enough.

In this mechanical civilization, the rational and limited intellect of the scientist is the only one that is respected. But it need not be so. It is the time to overcome the bifurcation of intellect; the time is approaching for religion and mysticism to take up the central rôle in the civilization that they possessed in the Middle Ages. Kierkegaard tried to make the Outsider's point of view look ponderous and academic in his attack on Hegel, the *Unscientific Postscript*. In doing this, he was more sensible than Blake, who launched his attack in long and murky 'prophecies' written in free verse. Even so, Kierkegaard made no impression on his own age. But today the outlook is changing. Heidegger has made Outsider-philosophy respected by the professors in Germany; Sartre and Camus did serious and influential work in France.

This revolution, although we hardly yet realize it, is one of the greatest events of our time. After four centuries, the tide is turning. The philosophers and artists have not only begun to assert that 'abstract philosophy' and scientific rationalism are inadequate; they have succeeded in restoring some degree of contact with the 'ordinary people'. Only in England and America—who are always behind the times—are the survivors of rationalism—Bertrand Russell, A. J. Ayer, Carnap—taken seriously. Existentialism is the philosophy of the *whole* human being—not merely of his reasoning intellect. And like religion and art, it recognizes that some human beings are wholler than others. Rationalism treats man as a mere spectator in the world, like a man in a cinema. He has nothing to do but look at the screen. Existentialism treats him as someone passionately involved, and with a destiny that is not merely social and economic.

Ouspensky wrote of Gurdjieff: 'His system belongs to that class of systems *which regard man as an incomplete being, and study him from the point of view of his possible development.*' This can be said of all Existentialism. Rationalism thinks of man essentially as a spectator of life. For Existentialism, he is 'involved'. For science, man is static. For Existentialism, he is dynamic.

Our way of thinking is swinging back to religion—which also regards man as involved. But then, Plato's thought was swinging back to religion too when Athens collapsed and Greek civilization began to decay. We have no cause for optimism. The problems involved in *whole nations* accepting a new religious attitude are too immense.

The function of religion is to keep before Man some purpose greater than his own petty preoccupations. Communism is a religion in this sense. It fails only because it is not broad enough; its dogmas are too limiting: 'Man is a social animal. Every man's sole duty is to the State.' Such a dogma might be useful in weeding out lazy and useless social parasites, and in bringing men of social purpose to the forefront; but a day would come when it would crush men of different purpose, the Outsiders. The aim of a religion is to give the maximum purpose to *all* men.

In his moments of deepest insight, the Outsider and the visionary knows that there is only one purpose: to intensify life, to create more vitality, to change men into supermen. In all his thinking, he begins from that point. He rejects mere social remedies —democracy, fascism, communism, anarchism—because he knows that they will not supply motive and purpose to the highest type of man for any length of time. He does not dismiss them; but he regards them as secondary. There must be greater aims than short-sighted social aims to fight for.

But where does one begin? It is said that when Sartre used to lecture after the war, his audiences left the lecture hall in a state of feverish inspiration, and a determination to change their lives. But Sartre had only told them to *be* more—to utilize their freedom; he had not explained what he wanted them to *do*. Their state of inspiration and determination never lasted for more than a few hours, in consequence. Gurdjieff made a greater effort; he prescribed all kinds of exercises and disciplines—even complicated Eastern dances—knowing that people need to make a radical alteration in their way of living; the only thing that distinguishes a religious purpose from any other purpose is its depth and permanence.

The answer points again to individual men: the Outsiders. I do not believe that there is any obvious and immediate measure to be taken—*except by the artists and writers*—especially the writers. The artist represents the highest consciousness of the age, and he attempts to extend that consciousness to other people. The first step: for the artists to become conscious of what has happened to our civilization since the days when the artist and law-giver were one. It demands, in other words, a historic consciousness on the part of writers. Secondly, and not less important, it demands a metaphysical consciousness (of the kind that Sartre proved he possessed in *La Nausée*, and Camus in *The Myth of Sisyphus*). This is the consciousness I tried to outline in *The Outsider*. The artist must cease to be the limp, impassive observer. He must become actively involved in the task of restoring a metaphysical consciousness to our age. This would be the first step to healing that 'bifurcation of nature' that Whitehead recognized to be the sign of our age's decay.

In the twentieth century there are three particular consequences of scientific materialism that must be combated. They are: neo-Darwinism in biology; Marxism in politics; logical positivism in philosophy.

Shaw has stated the objections to neo-Darwinism in his *Methuselah* preface, and conclusively demonstrated its fallacy. In his *Socialist Systems*, Wilfred Pareto revealed the naïveté of Marxian idealism. So far, unfortunately, no one has turned the machine gun on logical positivism. And yet logical positivism is no less vulnerable than the other two. The trouble seems to be that most metaphysicians—the natural enemies of the logical positivists—are too polite to hit out at the vulnerable spots of the logical positivists—or perhaps too unimaginative to see them clearly.

In the Middle Ages, philosophy was 'the handmaiden of theology'; philosophy meant a consideration of the relation of Man to God, or to life, or to the totality of the universe. Logical positivism cuts out one of these terms: 'Man'; and philosophy becomes the attempt to reach out towards 'truth' by means of logical analysis. The logical philosopher behaves as if he is inside a glass tank, looking out at 'life' from a perfectly detached standpoint, untouched by it all. The artist and the artist-philosopher (the existentialist) behave as if they are actively involved in life, and treat philosophy as a question about themselves as much as about the universe. 'Logical philosophy' calls upon science to justify its method, pointing out that science pushes the world to arm's length, and then analyses it. (They prefer to ignore the increasing tendency in modern physics to take the 'observer' into account; his importance in relativity physics and Heisenberg's uncertainty principle.) Philosophy is now the handmaiden of science and mathematics.

*   *   *

Our age is the age of the scientist. This in itself is not a bad thing. It is better than barbarism. I myself was trained as a physicist until I was seventeen, and have never ceased to be fascinated by physics and mathematics, although now I could not undertake to explain the binomial theorem to a schoolboy. I have always felt sympathy with the mentality of the scientist and mathematician. Consequently, my own existentialism has none of the Blakeian desire to abolish the scientific intellect. It is not the fault of the scientist that our age has become rotten with scientific materialism. It is the fault of the artists and religious men for not emphasizing the Outsider viewpoint to counteract it. This is the supremely cheering thing about this post-war age: the Outsider's viewpoint is again coming to its own. But it can only become dominant through the intellectual activity of creative artists. And since the ideal aim would be to again have the scientists accepting the religious viewpoint as intellectually tenable, it is only fair that the artists—the Outsiders—should be prepared to make an equal effort to comprehend the scientific intellect. If the Outsider is to be the representative figure of the twentieth century, he *must* comprehend it. The existentialist ideal is not a ' system of ideas ', but greater men. Again, the image of the scientist, who has to absorb the scientific tradition of four hundred years before he can begin to create his own work, is the image of the Outsider. All consciousness of the past must be summed up in him; he must be an ' encyclopedist ' whose breadth of knowledge is only an instrument of creation, a prerequisite of the wider consciousness he needs to create new mind.

I began this ' credo ' by stating that I intended to adopt a more personal approach than in my critical books; I have not been able to carry out this good resolution as far as I intended. Moreover, I have re-crossed my tracks several times; this is perhaps one of the penalties of trying to take the reader for a sleigh ride over the area of my working beliefs. The result may be vertiginous; so I hasten to attempt a summary for the benefit of any reader who is wondering what it all adds up to.

In past ages, the Outsider was the religious man and the rebel. The Church has always tended to swerve from its course, to compromise; then the Outsider is the man who refuses to compromise. Consider, for instance, the men whom I have treated in *Religion and the Rebel*: Waldo and Wycliffe, in revolt against the Catholic Church; Boehme, in revolt against protestantism (he called the

Church 'a spiritual whore-house'); Pascal, against Jesuitry (the most powerful form of the Church in seventeenth-century France); William Law, against broad-church liberalism; Newman, against contemporary Victorian humanism; Kierkegaard, against protestantism; Shaw, against scientific materialism (neo-Darwinism). All these men were rebels, and what they rebelled against was the spiritual current of the age (or perhaps I should say, its intellectual climate). As we come down to our own day, the Outsider is no longer the rebel against the spiritual current of the age; at least, that current is not embodied in anything he can revolt against. He is the 'rebel without a cause'. The anarchy of the age confuses him; it gives him no solid position from which to fire off his guns. He must begin by building such a position. When it is built, it is called Existentialism. Once upon a time, it would have been called religion.

But religion has a home—the Church. Existentialism has no home—yet.

The Outsider is the rebel in the spiritually anarchic civilization.

And yet the anarchy is essential. Anarchy is a mid-way stage between superstition and true conviction. It contains the seeds of new order. Societies become anarchic when the masses are half-educated. Half-education teaches scepticism, but not the power to hack through scepticism to a new belief. But scepticism is a necessary stage in a society's evolution. Most intelligently religious men go through a stage of atheism in their youth. But scepticism is uncreative; it must be transformed by continual searching into belief. So a society's scepticism must be transformed by a new religious belief. Religions are a response to a need of Outsiders in a sceptical civilization (or a civilization where the religion has become mere ritual).

A sceptical civilization is a half-dead civilization. In the past, civilizations have always collapsed at their sceptical stage. It is as if all religious men died in their early atheistic stage.

No civilization has ever yet achieved its possible maturity. They all pass through the same stages : simple superstitious belief to half-educated scepticism. But so far, no civilization has advanced to the next stage : the stage of a new religious belief based on religious vision, the Outsider's vision.

What would this involve?

Nothing less than the evolution of a higher type of man. For if every member of society were capable of somehow participating in the Outsider's religious attitude, the result would be a higher level of civilization than has ever yet been known to history; and its highest type of man would appear to us, in our present stage, as hardly less than superman.

A wild vision, perhaps; and yet our civilization now faces the challenge before which all previous civilizations have shown themselves inadequate: Produce a higher type of man, or smash.

But how could this challenge be met today? What is to be done? A new religion? World government? Platonic philosopher-kings?

For my own part, I must confess that I can see no clear road ahead. The answer cannot be drawn up neatly to specifications, like a problem in logic. I cannot talk in terms of 'we'; only in terms of 'I'. The need is to strive to deepen the consciousness of our position, to communicate a sense of urgency.

My own personal part in this involves hauling up the banner of existentialism. This may sound particularly inadequate, but it is all I can do as a writer. My particular bugbear is abstract philosophy, scientific materialism. For me, real philosophy is an attempt at an estimate of the human situation from the point of view of somebody involved in it; not abstruse questions of logic or metaphysics. Consequently, for me, the instrument of philosophy is not the huge metaphysical tract, but the personal journal, the case-book (like James's *Varieties of Religious Experience*)—or, best of all, the novel. Plato was an existentialist philosopher in the sense I mean; so was Goethe; both were as interested in human beings as in philosophy. Plato's *Symposium* is a sort of novel; Goethe's *Wilhelm Meister*, a sort of philosophical treatise. Existentialist philosophy reaches a climax in Tolstoy and Dostoevsky; the fundamental questions of human existence are debated *strictly in terms of human beings*. The ideal philosopher, then, is the artist-philosopher, the poet-philosopher (Rilke is a good example of this), the novelist-philosopher. The mere ' philosopher ' is a bloodless half-man; a contributory cause to the spiritual anarchy of our time. The work of the great ' abstract philosophers ' is of immense value, of course; the Kants, the Hegels, are not to be dismissed. But it is lop-sided, and its lop-sidedness threatens to sink us. And their genius for abstraction has run philosophy into the dead end of logical positivism and linguistics.

If I were asked to prescribe a rule that all future philosophers would have to obey, it would be this: That no idea shall be expressed that cannot be expressed in terms of human beings in a novel—and perfectly ordinary human beings at that—not Peacockian brain-boxes. If an idea cannot be expressed in terms of people, it is a sure sign it is irrelevant to the real problems of life. Logic and mathematics should be clearly recognized as *games*, to be confined to the classroom or the mental gymnasium; mere aids to philosophy. The philosophers who have devoted their lives to these games should not be classified with Plato and Goethe, but with W. G. Grace, Alex James and Henry Cotton.

It must be confessed that the artist-philosopher I have in mind has not yet come into existence: the greatest examples—Plato, Goethe, Tolstoy, Dostoevsky, are imperfect examples. Shaw, who is the only twentieth-century figure to compare to these giants, was no artist compared with Shakespeare, Balzac, Gogol. And yet Shaw, in many ways, comes closer to the ideal of the existentialist than Sartre, or Camus, or Marcel. His work is a continuous exploration of the Outsider problem, and he possesses a sense of history. And he realized that the job of the artist and of the philosopher is to widen the area of consciousness for the civilization. In *Man and Superman*, Tanner states: 'Our minds are but this knowledge of ourselves and he who adds a jot to such knowledge creates new mind as surely as any woman creates new men.' And in the preface of *Back to Methuselah*: 'I had always known that civilization needs a religion as a matter of life or death.' Just as each generation's scientists and mathematicians have more to learn before they begin their own work—just as a baby compresses thousands of years of evolution into the nine months before it is born—so, if civilization is to survive, men must develop a sense of purpose beyond the immediate demands of their everyday lives. The scientist who is a moral imbecile, the statesman whose ambitions are strictly personal, are of no use whatever to civilization, no matter how efficient one may be in his laboratory, and the other in the House of Commons. The qualities required for our survival are the moral qualities of the religious reformer or the Eastern sage: self-control and sense of purpose. And these qualities, which are so completely lacking in English literature today (and are not very evident on the Continent) must be restored if literature is not to degenerate into a machine-made article, technically efficient and acutely observed, but trivial.

This can only be done if the writers and artists adopt a common credo, as in former ages. The responsibility has never been heavier for the men who are capable of original thought. The Church has failed civilization. (That, of course, is not to say that it may not be the valid solution for many Outsiders—I am speaking of civilization generally.) A religious credo would seem to be impossible nowadays. But the sense of moral purpose, the sense of spiritual reality, reduced to its simplest formula, is an Outsider viewpoint, the viewpoint of a religious existentialism. Whether this sense could communicate itself to the civilization at large is anybody's guess—at this stage. That depends upon the men who try to communicate it.

They call

it cricket

JOHN OSBORNE

John Osborne

Born in 1929. His first play was produced when he was seventeen—he describes it as 'terrible'. A short spell of journalism which he forsook for the theatre as an actor. Two other plays had provincial production. As an actor, unknown in London, there were long periods of unemployment and during one of these he wrote *Look Back in Anger*. In 1956, with the Royal Court Theatre production of this play, he became famous overnight, and the play was bought for performance in New York and Paris, and at the Berlin Festival. He joined the English Stage Company as an actor, and in 1957 his next play, *The Entertainer*, was produced with Sir Laurence Olivier in the lead.

WHENEVER I sit down to write, it is always with dread in my heart. But never more than when I am about to write straightforward prose, because I know then that my failure will be greater and more obvious. There will be no exhilarating skirmishes, no small victories on the way to defeat. When I am writing for the theatre I know these small victories: when the light on my desk is too bright and my back aches, but I go on writing because I am afraid that my pen will lose the words that come into my head; when I watch an actor on an empty stage deliver something that proves to me that my sense of timing has been exact, after all. Timing is an artistic problem, it is the prime theatrical problem. You can learn it, but it cannot be taught. It must be felt. Things like this—composition, sonata form, the line that is unalterable—there are small victories to be won from them, because these are things that seem worth doing for themselves. If you are any good at all at what you set out to do, you know whether it is good and rely on no one to tell you so. You depend on no one.

It is not true to say that a play does not 'come alive' until it is actually in performance. Of course it comes alive—to the man who has written it, just as those three symphonies must have come alive to Mozart during those last six weeks. One is sure to fail, but there are usually enough perks to be picked up on the way to make it bearable. It is the pattern of life itself, and it is acceptable. But whenever I sit down to write in prose about my present feelings and attitudes, my dread is enormous because I know that there will be no perks to pick up, or if there are, that they will be negligible.

For years—ever since I started earning my living in the theatre —I have been having the same dream: I am about to make my entrance on the stage, and behind the flats I can hear the other actors performing a play I know nothing about. My entrance is important, but I don't know when to make it. I stand there, peering through the cracks in the scenery trying to find out what is going on. Eventually, I decide that I have missed my entrance long before, and grab the door handle and push. Everything rattles and I am suddenly in a world where I cannot see anything although the light is so bright. I don't know any of my moves, or even what my first line should be, but I make a great effort to speak, to say something. I open my mouth and drive all the strength I can find into my diaphragm. But I can make no sound. I try to force my eyelids open, and I can't. I can feel the light, but I can't see.

I have dreaded writing this piece. If I were ever capable of doing it, I am not capable of doing it now. Months ago some kind of weakness or vanity made me agree to contribute to this book, but I have procrastinated to the point of downright bad manners until I am now the only writer in this symposium who has not delivered his copy. They are all—apparently—waiting for me. I do not relish having to address myself to what is almost certain to be a self-conscious literary mob, people who write sneering, parochial stuff in the weekend reviews. I can't solve anybody else's problems, least of all these creatures', collecting their literary cocoa tin lids every week. The people I should like to contact —if I knew how—aren't likely to be reading this book anyway. If they have ever heard of me, it is only as a rather odd-looking 'angry young man'. Surprisingly enough, the posh political weeklies are less scrupulous than even the popular press about digging into the private lives of people like myself. When I say 'people like myself', I mean people who have been over-publicized because of something they have written, and made money out of. Almost always the first question I am asked by press men is, 'How much money have you made?' At least it is not quite so impertinent as 'What are you angry about?'

Part of my job is to try and keep people interested in their seats for about two-and-a-half hours; it is a very difficult thing to do, and I am proud of having been even fairly successful at it. *Look Back in Anger* has been playing to large audiences all over the country for months, at a time when touring is all but finished. Provincial audiences (who, on the whole, are far more receptive than West End audiences) don't remember what the posh papers said about plays, even if they read them. They go to the theatre because the guvnor's wife went on Monday night and said it was a jolly good show. I simply want to point out that my job has not been an easy one to learn, merely because I have had what looks like an easy success. I shall go on learning as long as there is a theatre standing in England, but I didn't learn the job from the *Daily Mail* or the *Spectator*.

I want to make people feel, to give them lessons in feeling. They can think afterwards. In some countries this could be a dangerous approach, but there seems little danger of people feeling too much—at least not in England as I am writing. I am an artist —whether or not I am a good one is beside the point now. For the first time in my life I have a chance to get on with my job, and that is what I intend to do. I shall do it in the theatre and, possibly, in films. I shall not try and hand out my gospel version of the Labour Party's next manifesto to prop up any journalist who wants a bit of easy copy or to give some reviewer another smart clue for his weekly written-up crossword game. I shall simply fling down a few statements—you can take your pick. They will be what are often called ' sweeping statements ', but I believe we are living at a time when a few ' sweeping statements ' may be valuable. It is too late for caution.

As I sit and write this, I can look back on a big week for the liars of Britain. It is only a few days since the Christmas Island explosion. And the cheap-jacks of Fleet Street have surpassed themselves in their efforts to make the most debased, criminal swindle in British history look like a great victory for common sense. ' It's Our H-Bomb!' yelled the *Daily Express* and went on to explain ' How We Fooled the Japs.' The Government, it was pointed out quite blandly, had deliberately misled everyone about the timing of the explosion so that the growing protests of the whole world were neatly dodged before they became unanswerable. At the bottom of this front page of bannered indecency was a column which was actually headed ' Six Hit for a Man Named Washbrook '—the man named Washbrook being a cousin of a well-known cricketer. The copywriters even managed to make it sound like cricket. As the *Daily Mail* put it, that was that. ' The argument about whether or not Britain should explode her H-Bomb is ended. It has vanished in a mushroom over the Central Pacific.' The following day, it printed a chatty piece about the wives of men who had made that mushroom. 'The H-Bomb Wives' it called them. There were photographs of them—Ordinary British House-wives. One of them was shown holding her baby. No one knows at this time whether one day some Japanese housewife may hold up a baby that is not quite so well-formed or healthy because of a few British husbands and their game of nuclear cricket.

The Tories, with all their old genius for self-deception and arrogance, had their game of cricket, and two days later they were able to wrap up the whole crime with the banner headline: 'The Duke—a T.V. Hit!' It is interesting, not because this line in sycophancy is unusual, but because it is, in fact, the kind you read in any newspaper on any day of the week. But this was a day in a very special week.

The Duke of Edinburgh had spoken to the children of the nation —to say nothing of their parents. Once again the *Mail* had the exact phrase—'it was unique.' There was a whole leading article devoted to the Duke's T.V. appearance. On any other day, this might have roused a smile from me, but I can't find the Duke of Edinburgh amusing much longer, any more than the Archbishop of Canterbury, Ephraim Hardcastle's debutantes, or Mr Macmillan.

Here are a few lines from the article; the following paragraph is headed 'Beauty'—quote:

'"I would like you to remember," he said [this is the Duke], "that all the people and the places you have seen belong to this family of nations of ours and I think it is worth remembering that we stick together not by force, but because we like each other." Simple words but true—and very precious in these times when so much that is unworthy and untrue is being spread about on the subject of British Imperialism. These words will have an even wider audience when the tele-recording of the talk is seen and heard in Canada and Australia, as they will be. If it goes to the United States, as it may do, perhaps our friends there will come to a better understanding of *what we stand for*. [Well, we'd shown them how to keep a straight bat, two days before, in the Pacific, hadn't we?] It won't be the first time in the present reign that such a thing has happened. The televised recordings of the Coronation showed the world not only the beauty of the ceremonial, but the essential spirituality of the rite.'

I can't go on laughing at the idiocies of the people who rule our lives. We have been laughing at their gay little madnesses, my dear, at their point-to-points, at the postural slump of the well-off and mentally under-privileged, at their stooping shoulders and strained accents, at their waffling cant, for too long. They are no longer funny, because they are not merely dangerous, they are murderous. I don't think I want to make people laugh at them any more because they are stupid, insensitive, unimaginative beyond hope, uncreative and murderous. I, too, have done nothing. I was furious with unbelief, but I went on going to work, answering my correspondence and talking to my friends. I behaved like any other 'intellectual' of my generation. We sat at home, well-fed, with our reputations and our bank-accounts intact, and left it to some hard-up little Unitarian who was over sixty to hitch-hike all the way, making the only gesture on his own. Nobody laughed at us, we made quite sure of that. 'H-Bomb Harold' the brave lads of Fleet Street called him. No doubt he was a crank, or he may not have been very smart or intelligent, but he was the only one of us who had the decency or the courage to leave his wife and children, take his savings out of the bank and make his comical little protest that was certain to fail. The liars in Westminster saw to that, the liars in Fleet Street saw to it. We 'intellectuals' saw to it, with our 'campaigns' and our signatures. During the Suez Crisis I had collected signatures to a letter to *The Times*! That was the limit of my imagination then. True, it was a very militant letter, possibly seditious even, which may have been the reason why it was not published. This time I didn't even send a letter to *The Times*. A writer can demonstrate feeling. It takes an extraordinary human being to demonstrate action as well. Most weeks, my own courage allowance doesn't last beyond Monday lunch-time.

Elgar and elegy, elegy and eulogy!

Nigel Dennis sent this sort of national swill through the roof in *Cards of Identity*. Admittedly, he hadn't thrown in an H-Bomb as well, but hardly anybody understood the significance of the point he was making. Or if they did, they thought it was amusingly impious but irrelevant and bumbled out the usual stock words like ' construction'; and ignored the fact that this play made more serious comments on our society—and made them with wit—than any English play that has appeared for years. Yet, *The Chalk Garden*, that doddering apotheosis of the English theatrical decadence of the last thirty years, had a few weeks before actually received serious critical attention. But then, having endowed a more or less permanent Old Ladies Home in the Haymarket, the London critics showed that most members of their own particularly peculiar Identity Club found themselves more in touch with the leader-writer of the *Daily Mail* than with Mr Dennis.

I have called Royalty religion the 'national swill' because it is poisonous, what an old vegetarian I used to know would call ' foodless food', or, as Orwell might have put it, the leader-writers and the bribed gossip mongers have only to rattle their sticks in the royalty bucket for most of their readers to put their heads down in this trough of Queen-worship, their tails turned against the world. It just doesn't seem so funny any more.

When my play *The Entertainer* was produced, it was complained that one of the characters was ' vaguely anti-queen'. Now, if this character was vague in the way she expressed herself, it was because the existence of the Lord Chamberlain's office compelled it. I should have been delighted if she could have been more explicit, although, in this case, I was anxious that this particular point should not be made too literally. The bigger point that this character was trying to make was something like: ' What kind of symbols do we live by? *Are* they truthful and worthwhile?' But in expressing herself in anti-queen terms, which was a relevant and colourful image—or so I thought—I believe she was asking an important question. I still believe it to be an important question.

Recently I read an article by David Marquand called 'Lucky Jim and the Labour Party'. It was an enjoyable article, in spite of its 'weekend' title, and the usual parasitic assumptions that go with these kinds of factitious equations. However, while reviewers continue to make a living out of it, equations like 'Lucky Jim

Plus' are as useful to them as 'Angry Y.M. Plus Miss X' is to the popular press. It also saves them the trouble of writing with wit, or of going in for a little original creation themselves—say, sitting down to write a suave, disengaged novel called, perhaps, *Orderly Roderick*, in which there would be nothing more than an occasional half smile of an emotional nuance like: 'After all, there *is* something to be said for civilization, isn't there?—Or isn't there?'

Well, the principal figures in this equation seem to have been Kingsley Amis, John Wain—and myself. A great deal of the L.J. gibberish has been promoted by a few words I put into the mouth of Jimmy Porter. These were: 'There aren't any good, brave causes left.' Immediately they heard this, all the shallow heads with their savage thirst for trimmed-off explanations got to work on it, and they had enough new symbols to play about with happily and fill their columns for half a year. They believed him, just as some believed Archie Rice when he said: 'I don't feel a thing' or 'I may be an old pouf, but I'm not right-wing.' They were incapable of recognizing the texture of ordinary despair, the way it expresses itself in rhetoric and gestures that may perhaps look shabby, but are seldom simple. It is too simple to say that Jimmy Porter himself believed that there were no good, brave causes left, any more than Archie didn't feel a thing.

At this I can hear all kinds of impatient inflections. 'Well, if your characters only mean what they say some of the time, when are we supposed to know what they're getting at? What are *you* getting at? What do you *mean*? How do you *explain* these characters, these situations?' At every performance of any of my plays, there are always some of these deluded pedants, sitting there impatiently, waiting for the plugs to come singing in during natural breaks in the action. If the texture is too complex, they complain that too much is going on for them to follow. There they sit, these fashionable turnips, the death's heads of imagination and feeling, longing for the interval and its over-projected drawls of ignorance. Like the B.B.C. critics, they either have no ear at all, or they can never listen to themselves.

I offer no explanations to such people. All art is organized evasion. You respond to Lear or Max Miller—or you don't. I can't

teach the paralysed to move their limbs. Shakespeare didn't describe symptoms or offer explanations. Neither did Chekhov.
Neither do I.

I have been continually expected to account for myself as if I
had committed some ghastly indiscretions, and to defend a position which I have never taken up. In fact, ' What these young men
are most angry about is that they have nothing on which to focus
their anger,' says Mr Marquand in his article. Here are these
demented, wretched chaps thrashing about, wasting their energies,
looking for something to be angry about and crying their hearts
out over it. What an embarrassing, tedious spectacle! Er, miss!
Miss! Dear, what *is* the woman doing! Two more gins and tonics.
Please! *Do* you mind! What a *bore* this is! Thank heavens I don't
have to write it up this evening!

It is a little unfair to credit these inflections to Mr Marquand
because his article is quite intelligent and sympathetic, but he has
fallen into many of the traps laid by the second-interval
intellectuals.

Mr Marquand says some good things, among them : ' If ossification and lack of imagination are the marks of decadent civilization
then for decadence this country must rival ancient Byzantium.' I
couldn't quarrel with that. Then he goes on : 'To remedy this
situation, revolutionary changes will be needed. And it is essential
that the changes necessary are clearly thought out *before* the
Labour Party comes to power; they cannot be adumbrated *ad hoc*
when Labour is already in office. Thus, the real task of the Party
in the next few years is thinking and planning. For this, Lucky
Jim is unfitted. The chaos of contemporary Britain can only be
cleared away by social salvage units, not *neurotic misfits cut off
from Society*.' Mr Marquand sounds like an ex-Party member at
times, and it is no surprise to hear him throw down a phrase like
this one.

Now, I have only met Mr Amis once briefly, and I have never
met Mr Wain, nor any of the rest of these poor successful freaks.
I have no idea whether they are either neurotic misfits or cut off
from society; but it doesn't seem likely. How is anyone ' cut off
from society '? Do you stop working, making love, having children, paying rates and taxes, making friends, reading newspapers

and books, walking in the street, having conversations, being ill?
Cut off from *what* society? Even in jail you become part of a
'society'. Mr A. and Mr W.—your old favourites and mine—
surely enter into a social relationship every time they walk into
their lecture rooms? And when does one become a neurotic misfit? To some people, a man who shouts obscenities when he
catches his finger in a door is a wildly unbalanced creature. It
isn't such a very long stop from calling people neurotic misfits to
telling them where they've got to live and work, and, ultimately,
piling them on to death wagons.

Some people needed to have the full meaning of lunatic indict-
ments like 'decadent formalism' spelled out for them in Budapest.
Not that it seems likely there were more than one or two
neurotic misfits around at that time. If there were, they probably
walked into a Russian tank on their way to the brothel or the
psychiatrist's or wherever it is that such weirdies eke out the
unproductive agony of their existence. Of course Robespierre and
Lenin were both 'intellectuals' but, we are told, ' *It is doubtful if
they had time to be neurotic.*'

I have singled out Mr Marquand's article because like so many
of those who speak from the 'let's all take off our jackets and get
down to it' Left, he shares the same assumptions about writers and
artists, as people who write articles about 'How to Make Your
First Fifty-Thousand.' He assumes that neurotic misfits sit at home
all day, and, apart from turning out the odd novel or play, hurl
things at their wives, sneer at their children, abase themselves
before their mistresses and lie fornicating and drinking gin, dream-
ing about money and lost revolutions, like pampered, hysterical
prize boars, flopping and charging about in the dung of their own
making. All the while the 'social salvage units' are quietly getting
on with the job, clearing away the chaos and the dirt, until that
day, when all the chaos and dirt that is left will be in the piggeries
of a few neurotic misfits. And when that time comes, perhaps they
will grunt and swill and squeal their last, for they will no longer
be useful to the social salvage units.

Because we *are* useful. The salvage units keep popping their
heads over the wall to see how we are getting on, measuring the
state of the stink and sewage we are producing, watching our

behaviour. Prod him with a stick—see if he grunts again! Oh, chuck that brick at him—he hasn't squealed for half an hour. Look at him, he's rolling in it again. It's dripping from his eyes now, he can't even see. My God, I know we have to keep them just now, but they *really are* pretty disgusting! All right lads, back to your units! Back to your *activity*. Your *productive* activity!

When you start describing people as neurotic misfits you are drawing on the language of psychiatry. But according to this language, what very often betrays the prize neurotic is his intense *productive* activity. Indeed, it was suggested a long time ago that this energy is, in fact, a social outlet for the deep-rooted anal preoccupations of busy, constructive people. If you accept this kind of analysis,—when you start calling people ' neurotic misfits' you finish up with the idea that there are no revolutions, only Napoleon and Henry Ford—or, yes, Robespierre and Lenin— busily staring down the lavatory pan. It is no use Lucky J. trying to imitate these admirable oozlem birds, these social salvage units. He just can't get his head down into that position at all. If he tried to take a hand in politics at the moment, ' he would either waste his time, or ours.' Notice that ' ours'. Reading this, I begin to feel safely locked up in my piggery already. ' He would either try vainly to recreate the atmosphere of the thirties, growing desper- ately dispirited in the process '—snort from the piggery: They've been peering over the wall again—wish they'd let me have a bit more rubbish to roll in—' or he would try successfully '—social salvage units here again, Leeds Group, Section One—' and steer left-wing politics on to the wrong track.'

I don't know what the wrong track is, and Mr Marquand doesn't say. Perhaps he is thinking of the track of a Russian tank, which is what made him withdraw from his last S.S.U. Old Lucky Jim may be a simple, romantic old snorter, but it didn't take him until last October to smell that one out. ' So all that is left is the sterile carping that he already indulges in. But is this altogether so sterile as it looks? On the surface, certainly there can have been few more futile forms of literature. The Aunt Sallies being bombarded are so *pitifully unimportant* [my italics]: Mozart, good manners, con- ventional religion, academic insulation from the world, the drab- ness of the Welfare State. This criticism forgets *that it is precisely on this pitiful, trivial level that people live* [my italics again].

It is difficult to make out whether ' people' means the S.S.U. or the piggeries. Are we to believe that a few *people* get locked in with these creatures, and are actually sloshing about in all that pitifully unimportant muck too? My God, we must get them out —mind you though, it may not be such a bad thing after all. Once they've had a good wash-down with a disinfectant hose, think how useful they could be to the S.S.U. Yes, why not! Lock 'em in the piggeries for a bit. Won't do any harm. Once they've been in, they won't want to go back. Rub their noses in a little conventional religion—it soon comes off afterwards, but it teaches them to appreciate a stink. Later on, when they come out, they can get to work on the real, important stinks. The S.S.U. will teach them. The drabness of the Welfare State? Yes, that'll do. The Queen? Yes, I suppose so, but you'll need some pepper. It'll probably only make them sneeze. Look, the pigs are showing them how to do it! Go on pigs, roll, flop over on your back in it, Lucky! Squeal, Jimmy, put your head down, slither away, or we won't let you have your swill today! The S.S.U. is fattening you up, isn't it? We want to look after you! Well, go on then—show them what you are—*pigs!*

What is surprising is that anyone should expect creatures who spend their lives in piggeries of their own making, even to consider leaving them. It is the only way they *can* live successfully. Why should anyone expect him to join his local S.S.U., let alone be a leading light in it, when he is so good at making smells and dirt at home?

I know that Mr Marquand is right when he says that we Lucky Jims will never be good S.S.U. members. I wouldn't. My place is in the piggery and I know it, much as I may often long to leave it. I have been there all my life. I expect to live there until I die. I don't believe that anyone should want me to leave it. I didn't get out of it during Suez and *do* anything. I didn't get out last week. I stayed where I was. Who knows, I may put my nose out now and then and get in everybody's way. But I know in my heart that the S.S.U. will recruit from politicians, social scientists, teachers, philosophers, psychologists, economists, all the professional Sanitary Inspectors, the sewage cleaners, the smell-killers. The place for a writer is his piggery—it's the place for me. He can make all the dung and smells there he likes.

This brings me back to the character in my play, the one who makes a vague anti-queen smell. Obviously, anyone who believes that what people feel about Jesus or the way they work and spend their leisure in the 'drabness of the Welfare State' is pitifully unimportant, will believe the same about Royalty religion. I do not apologize for choosing to attack personalities who 'are not in a position to defend themselves.' Surely anyone, however remote from the facts of reasonably normal experience, must tire occasionally of the everlasting noise of mooing? Besides, the worker priests of Fleet Street are not likely to let pass any attack on the rock of their foundation. If they were deprived of their daily opportunity to conduct mass worship of supreme nonentities, they might even be forced one day to start picking at the scabs of reality instead.

People need symbols to live by, they need a kind of rough behaviour pattern to follow. This we all know. Unlike the Church, most ordinary English people are more concerned with behaviour than belief. Quite sensibly, they have always believed, not in justification by faith, but by works. Almost always the first objection of the English protestant or atheist to Catholicism is the concept of confession. The idea of coming out with all sorts of embarrassing stuff to some chap who, when all is said and done, is no better than the rest of us, offends his common sense and his sense of democracy. One cannot ever imagine an English protestant being persuaded to confess his sins, even to a royal personage. The idea that sleeping with someone else's spouse may be overlooked, provided you believe in God and tell the Duke all about it in the morning, would stick in the throat of even the most ardent royalist.

During the past fifty years, the Church has repeatedly ducked every moral issue that has been thrown at its head—poverty, unemployment, fascism, war, South Africa, the H-Bomb, and so on. It has lived in an atmosphere of calm, casual funk. It has not been entirely negative in its attitude. It has even managed to spread the gospel of funk. With its village quarrels about divorce and remarriage, and its favourite topic—the reimbursement of the clergy—its capacity for self-mockery seems to have been unlimited. Its bishops have sounded like bewigged old perverts at Assizes. There has never been one outstanding moral issue on which the Church has taken a firm, unequivocal stand for simple, social decency, let alone for the Gospel. After half a century of watching groups of wealthy theologians publicly turning their back on Jesus, the British public slowly began to realize that the bishops were just playing another word game, like the politicians.

People grew accustomed to the fact that 'we must all pull together for the common good' turned out to mean for the good of those who said it. They came to expect to be lied to and gypped by them. In fact they were so accustomed to it that often they failed to recognize the thieves' language of Westminster—even when they bothered to read it. They became numbed by parliamentary patois that urged in moments of crisis 'that no decision should be taken,' that spoke of tragedy as a matter for 'grave concern', that commented upon a disastrous debacle, that there were indications that 'the situation is in hand.'

It began to dawn upon the nation that the religion game was just as meaningless as the politics game, that the spiritual spiel of the wide boys of the Church was not simply a smooth confidence trick of trained hereditary rulers which could be admired for its sheer dexterity, but was also a betrayal of the very future of civilization. When Peter denied Jesus he said: 'I do not know the man.' When bishops speak, they begin: 'While seeking not to deny the claims of subject peoples to ultimate self-realization we do not feel that we can attempt to interfere in the affairs . . .' But the Church has had two thousand years in which to work out a language that makes murder sound like charity. In England it simply had not been called upon for some time to use it with quite the barefaced subtlety with which it had been uttered throughout the rest of Europe.

Every day on the radio, in the press and on television, the Church hawked around its Jesus Figure like a vacuum cleaner, but nobody felt inclined to buy a machine that not only failed to beat, sweep or clean, but actually made a nice mess as well. It had *JESUS* written on the bag, but the bag contained only the air of another bunch of overpaid liars. When the Jesus jingles came on,

75

most people simply switched off their responses automatically, and waited for the next programme. They knew that the people selling the product were themselves utterly incapable of making the damned thing *work*. They behaved exactly like the people who were selling something else, or who, better still, weren't selling anything at all. Like so many other English Institutions, the Church was beginning to lose its comic value.

People are too bored by parsons to laugh at them any more. It is well known that often the funniest thing a comic can do is *not* do it, but the Church has over-worked this moral gag so much and for so long that it goes on playing to the numbers that such a miserable act deserves. People turned to other acts that could at least be relied upon to give the advertised performance. James Dean and Marilyn Monroe did good business. They were obviously genuine, they *worked*: you got your money's worth, they could be imitated. Was there an English act that could top the bill, that could be relied on to fill all sections of the house? There was—it wasn't a very new act, but it was well organized, and completely brought up to date: that fabulous family we all love so well—the Amazing Windsors!

My objection to the Royalty symbol is that it is dead; it is the gold filling in a mouthful of decay. While the cross symbol represented *values*, the crown simply represents a *substitute* for values. When the Roman crowds gather outside St Peter's, they are taking part in a moral *system*, however detestable it may be. When the mobs rush forward in the Mall they are taking part in the last circus of a civilization that has lost faith in itself, and sold itself for a splendid triviality, for the 'beauty of the ceremonial' and the 'essential spirituality of the rite'. We may not create any beauty or exercise much spirituality, but by God! we've got the finest ceremonial and rites in the world! Even the Americans haven't got that.

Ever since a generation thrilled to an announcer intoning the lines about its king's life moving peacefully to its close, the B.B.C. has produced a staff of highly-trained palace lackeys with grave-yard voices, and a ponderous language stuffed with Shakespearian and semi-Biblical echoes. It is all as nourishing and useful as wax fruit under a glass case. But to a nation that finds her most significant myths in the idiot heroes of *Reach for the Sky* and *Battle of the River Plate* and longs for aggrandizement but cannot afford a new set of teeth or a breast plate that will save her from humiliation, it is about the one wholly satisfying thing left.

Because royalty is deprived of active political power, and therefore of the necessity to make moral, or any other, decisions, it is presented with a staggering power that gives it a greater grip on the public imagination than any other single institution. Whilst commanding a unique position, it is protected from ever having to attempt to solve a problem or make a choice. It is not merely above criticism, it is above the necessity of having to justify its existence. It is unhealthy because it encourages a peculiarly sloppy-cynical attitude to politics.

Nobody can seriously pretend that the royal round of gracious boredom, the protocol of ancient fatuity, is politically useful or morally stimulating—the state visits to countries like France and Portugal which successfully fulfil the monarchy function of disguising important political issues—such as the barbarity of the French Government's policy in Algeria, and the openly anti-democratic constitution of Portugal—in a sludge of generalized patriotic feelings. As for the ship launchings, the visits to 'establishments', the polo games, the night-clubs with well-bred nobodies, the T.V. appearances, the endless concentration at the racecourse, the Christmas Day set-cant: are these the crowning interests of a rich, healthy culture? Is no one aghast at the thought of a lifetime of reading about the first day at prep-school, the measles, the first dance, the wedding, and finally the beauty of *the* ceremonial?

It bores me, it distresses me that there should be so many empty minds, so many empty lives in Britain to sustain this fatuous industry; that no one should have had the wit to laugh it into extinction, or the honesty to resist it. I don't believe that there can be one intellectual in the Labour Party who doesn't find it hilarious or contemptible. Naturally they would never dream of losing all those votes by saying so, but as long as they encourage people to revel in the political and literal horseplay of a meaningless symbol, they need not expect the masses to start discovering meanings in a serious political idea like socialism. A socialist party that is not republican is not crediting its potential followers with reason or intelligence. By suggesting to a man that fatuity, as long as it is hallowed by tradition, is acceptable and admirable, you cannot expect him to treat a complex social concept with any seriousness. He is not conditioned to seriousness but to totem worship. Whilst a ridiculous anachronism is reverenced as a serious institution the road to socialism will be bedevilled by regard for implicit ruling-class ideals like 'restraint', 'good taste', 'healthy caution' and so on.

It is not easy for ordinary people to liberate themselves from these ideals. They are not encouraged to. When a writer like myself tries to take a tilt at them, he is invariably misunderstood because he is interpreted almost entirely by people sodden in the culture-mores of Oxford and Cambridge, whose knowledge of working-class or sub-middle-class life is confined to second-hand observation, 'social studies', and all the microscope-peering and equations that go with them.

One of the difficulties in the way of trying to establish a 'working' culture is the stupidity of most critics, who mis-interpret one's intentions, partly from insensibility, but also from simple, unacknowledged ignorance. However, it is too much to expect any of them to get up and admit that they have never lived in a street where the lavatories are all 'outside'. Or even spoken for half an hour to anyone who has. Naturally, no writer can be expected to have 'experienced' all the things he reads and watches, any more than an actor can have experienced all his rôles. Most of the time they must rely on an imaginative intuition. But while this quality remains so rare a little quiet personal surveying in the large light hours before the curtain rises would do no harm. An actor successfully cast as a dock worker need not necessarily have done a day's physical work in his life. At the same time, if he were reasonably conscientious, he would certainly get down to some hard, on-the-spot observing, 'getting the feel of it'. All of this might be pretty superficial, but it would at least be an attempt at understanding.

Most good actors have the humility to admit when they are floundering in the dark. There are few critics who would not be better for the same dose of honesty in their morning tea. But then

you can't be expected to know much about art if most of your
time has been spent in assessing art that is scarcely on speaking
terms with the facts of life as known and felt by the great mass of
people in Britain today. True, there have been detectable signs of
a willingness to learn, and pious expressions about 'real people
and real emotions' have been uttered in all kinds of unlikely
quarters. So much so, that when *Summer of the Seventeenth
Doll* was presented in London, there was a stampede of middle-
class converts wanting to baptize themselves in the sweat of the
common man. People who would be simply incapable of com-
municating successfully—or wanting to—for ten minutes with a
road sweeper in Nottingham or a bus conductor in Bristol, assured
us that here was 'the authentic quality and feel' of the kind of
people who had never possessed a cheque book or a store account.
The play was excitingly conceived but its execution did not bring
to mind Tennessee Williams so much as the authors of *Sailor
Beware*. *Death of a Salesman* is not a play about commercial
travellers but this seemed to me to be a play about cane cutters,
although I am prepared to believe that its impact would have
been greater if it had been more than indifferently performed.

It is an inescapable fact that when the middle classes discuss
experience that is not dominated by their own emotional values,
they hedge and bluster with all they've got. A few weeks ago,
a reviewer wrote: 'One is compelled to believe that if they [the
characters] have indeed been drawn from life, Mr Osborne has set
them down with shamelessly pointed accuracy.' This, at least, is
refreshingly honest. There is no pretence at being capable of
judging whether the characters have been indeed drawn from
life—just a shrug at shamelessly pointed accuracy. The boys in
the orchestra at the Royal Court Theatre were capable of judging,
and they did: '*We've been through it and we know what it is
like*.' This is what audiences have muttered beneath their heart-
beat as they have watched Oedipus or Lear or Willie Loman. 'It's
still a bitter truth of life,' says the same writer, 'that the most
wretched human beings become bores when they start moaning—
even the sick, the aged and afflicted.' This sentence sums up fairly
neatly a prevalent class attitude to the pain and struggle of other
people. I do not accept it for one moment. It is true that the

C*

middle classes do not talk about their private troubles. But like working people they do moan a great deal about the way they think they are being cheated out of their inheritance, submerged by taxes and unfair checks on their 'incentive'—in other words they are not allowed to make enough money to buy themselves their traditional privileges—the education that will assure them of the best places in the sun. But, on the whole, they scrupulously avoid discussing their personal problems. Even with their friends.

I remember a very charming, middle-aged lady almost in tears as she told me that because of the Labour Government she was now forced to live on forty pounds a week. To her, it was a real disturbing problem, and she almost lost her temper because I was bad-mannered enough to let her see that I found it comic. Social injustice that spelled out £2000 a year didn't look like any problem to me. I pointed out that my mother and I had lived on 22s. 6d. a week at one time. But she looked at me as if I had opened my mouth and nothing had happened. At this period in my life, this kind of response had not become an occupational normality for me, and I was quite baffled. No doubt, she regarded my irrelevance about how people lived on 22s. 6d. as a 'shamelessly pointed accuracy'.

I should have known better, for I had always been made acutely aware of this class stonewall in my own family. My mother's parents were publicans—to be accurate, they managed a succession of pubs in London—until my grandfather 'lost it all'. My mother has worked behind the bar most of her life. She still does because she likes to 'be with other people'. Her own mother, who is now eighty-four, retired a few years ago on a small pension from Woolworths. (If I were to put a detail like that into a play, some bright social observer would be certain to wave me aside: 'One of its strange weaknesses is the apparent wrongness of its sociological facts. For example, one often found oneself wondering if the old woman wasn't merely an intellectual idea sketchily worked out rather than *felt*—that pension, surely we all know . . .') She is a tough, sly old Cockney, with a harsh, often cruel wit, who knows how to beat the bailiffs and the money-lenders which my grandfather managed to bring on to her. Almost every working day of her life, she has got up at five o'clock to go out to work, to walk down what has always seemed to me to be the most hideous and coldest street in London. Sometimes when I have walked with her, all young bones and shiver, she has grinned at me, her face blue with what I thought was cold. 'I never mind the cold—I like the wind in my face.' She'd put her head down, hold on to her hat and *push*.

The whole family pushed, and whenever they got together for some celebration, there would be plenty to drink, however hard things were. That alone is something middle-class people find difficult to understand or forgive. As a small boy I would be given 'a little drop of port', and sit apprehensively always, while my grandfather told me about *The Bells* and bawled bits of the Bible at me. He was the only man I had met until I was in my late teens who used a cigarette holder. He was stylish and impressive in the way he could roll out names—Sir Edward Carson, the Prince of Wales, Lord Rosebery, the Lord Chief Justice, the Aga Khan ('Mum always likes me to put a shilling on the black man's horses,' my mother would say). Lord Beaverbrook was a particular favourite because he had seen him once, emerging from his Rolls Royce. 'One of the finest men in England today!' He seemed to know everything about him. 'When I was with Beaverbrook during that time . . .' He had worked as a canvasser in the north of England for the *Daily Express*. I would sit flushed with port and embarrassment while he told me that he would live to see the day when I would be Prime Minister of England.

During all this, the rest of the family would be yelling news to each other. A lot of it would be about some illness or other. My grandmother would come in and out of the kitchen, usually picking the wrong moments to interrupt my grandfather—I would be the only one listening to him, but then I was the only one who seemed to listen to anybody. They didn't talk to each other so much as to themselves. He would yell some humiliation or if she was sitting near enough kick her imperceptibly but efficiently under the table. Often if I could escape, I would follow her into the scullery and get a slice of the 'dinner', some winks, and possibly some story about how my grandfather had spent a week-end with some famous music-hall artist at Brighton. She told a story like this with some pride, but I would know that she was scoring off him too. 'Course *he* doesn't know we know about it.' It must have eased the pain in her shin bone.

By dinner-time—which meant about two o'clock in the afternoon—the emotional temperature would be quite high. There would be baffling shrieks of laughter, yelling, ignoring, bawling, everyone trying to get his piece in. A big celebration would be the worst, like Christmas, when there was invariably a row. Sometimes there would be a really large gathering, and we would all go over to Tottenham, which was the family headquarters.

Setting out from South London, it was an exciting journey. One never knew what might happen. There would be two or three dozen of us—somebody's brother would have a pint too many at the pub and perhaps hit his wife; carnation button holes would be crumpled; there would be tears and lots and lots of noise. The day would end up with someone—usually my father—at the piano and everyone shouting songs at each other. They bawled and laughed and they moaned. There was rivalry in the way they spoke about how hard they worked and there was no question that they did work hard—about the visits to the hospital and the *waiting*. They 'talked about their troubles' in a way that would embarrass my middle-class observer. I've no doubt that they were often boring, but life still had meaning for them. Even if they did get drunk and fight, they were responding; they were not defeated.

My father's family were baffled by them. Their value system was quite different. What impressed me most when I was a small boy about my other grandparents, and all my father's relatives, was the calm that surrounded them. Not only were their voices soft, but they actually *listened* to what you were saying. They came from South Wales and cared for the language they spoke. Not that I am suggesting that this is a ruling pattern among middle-class people, but most of their bawling seems to be done in *public* places, like theatres and restaurants—less at home. Besides, my father and all his family were particularly gentle. There were no fights, few rows, hardly ever tears. Whenever there was an argument, it was nearly always about *income* and mostly characterized by gravity and long stretches of silence.

My grandparents were the poorest members of the family— Grandfather had spent too much time away from his jewellery business, playing cricket. This may seem unlikely, and I shouldn't care to have to 'explain' it in good old competent working-dramatist terms, but it is the literal truth. My grandmother's attitude to his cricket was rather similar to that of my other grandmother's attitude to weekends with famous music hall artists. My father had worn his cousin's cast-off Eton suits, and there hadn't been a cook or maid in the house since the first World War.

They were kind charming people, and I was deeply fond of them. I used to enjoy the time I spent there—which was a great deal—much more than that I spent with my relations in Fulham and Tottenham. They had a sense of fun which was as much a part of their assumption about life as their simple expectation that they should be waited on, that their children should go to public schools, that there should always be 'income'.

One day I was walking with my grandfather, when we were passed by a man who seemed to greet him rather cheerfully. He was answered with a curtness that was surprising for a man as gentle as my grandfather. 'That man's a socialist,' said my grandfather. I knew it couldn't be good from the quiet way he said it. He looked at me, and smiled. 'That's a man who doesn't believe in raising his hat.' That definition served me for a long time.

I am not going to define my own socialism. Socialism is an experimental idea, not a dogma; an attitude to truth and liberty, the way people should live and treat each other. Individual definitions are unimportant. The difference between Socialist and Tory values should have been made clear enough by this time. I am a writer and my own contribution to a socialist society is to demonstrate those values in my own medium, not to discover the best ways of implementing them. I don't need to step outside my own home to canvass for the Labour Party. Years ago, T. S. Eliot wrote: 'In a society like ours, worm-eaten with Liberalism, the only thing possible for a person with strong convictions is to state a point of view and leave it at that.' Substitute Toryism for Liberalism, and I'd say that this very roughly sums up my present socialist attitude—an experimental attitude to feeling. All the fields of experiment must be tackled by their own experts—economists and sociologists, town planners and educationists, industrial psychologists, observers, lawmakers and truth seekers.

Nobody can be very interested in my contribution to a problem like the kind of houses people should have built for them, the kind of school they should send their children to, or the pensions they should be able to look forward to. But there are other questions to be asked—how do people live inside those houses? What is their relationship with one another, and with their children, with their neighbours and the people across the street, or on the floor above? What are the things that are important to them, that make them care, give them hope and anxiety? What kind of language do they use to one another? What is the meaning of the work they do? Where does the pain lie? What are their expectations? What moves them, brings them together, makes them speak out? Where is the weakness, the loneliness? Where are the things that are unrealized? Where is the strength? Experiment means asking questions, and these are all the questions of socialism.

What is our answer to circulation-builders like 'How To Make a Hundred Thousand Pounds'? No one who believes in a just, decent society can be interested in a solution which can, after all, only result in a dubious happiness for a few people. Most of us can, at the moment, confidently expect to live at a reasonably comfortable material level, but very few of us can be rich. What kind of energy is it that is directed principally on behalf of good old number one? Is it productive, is it creative, rich? *Is* it going to make us happy?

Are we going to continue to be fooled by a class of inept deceivers, are we going to go on being ruled by them? They *are* inept and they always have been because they are incapable of recognizing a problem. What made Suez a typically Tory venture was not only its deception, its distaste for the basic assumptions of democracy, but the complete ineptitude of its execution. They will never learn; they will always be busy propping up the same totems, organizing their number one worship. Now when the techniques of communication are almost boundless, there has never seemed to be so little to say to one another, or so little desire to say it. It could be an exciting, creative time, so let the scribblers scratch, and let England bleed; there will be singing one day. I hope so; I look forward to it. Somebody's fingers must be itching?

Along
the tightrope

JOHN WAIN

John Wain

Born 1925 in Stoke-on-Trent, Staffordshire. Educated locally and at St John's College, Oxford. Began as an academic (Fereday Fellow of St John's, Lecturer in English Literature at Reading University), but found the double *métier* increasingly difficult, and in December 1955 resigned to become free-lance author and literary critic. At present engaged on a clutch of three novels, the first of these being *The Contenders*, publication spring 1958. Hopes to write for the theatre and, if opportunity occurs, for films. Says that he does not intend to give up writing poetry and criticism and that his other work will have to be arranged so as to leave some time over for these. Publications include: *Hurry On Down* and *Living in the Present* (novels); *Mixed Feelings* and *A Word Carved on a Sill* (poetry); a volume of criticism, *Preliminary Essays*; an anthology, *Contemporary Reviews of Romantic Poetry*; and a symposium of essays on poems, *Interpretations*.

The world is only the mirror of ourselves. If
it's something to make one puke, why then
puke, me lads, it's your own sick mugs you're
looking at!—HENRY MILLER

THE writer's subject-matter, the thing all
literature is *about*, can be indicated very simply : it is about what
it is like to be a human being. Everybody has his own view of
what constitutes humanity, and this view determines his actions
and attitudes; if he is an artist, it determines what kind of art he
produces. Authors fall into two categories, broadly speaking : those
whose concern with humanity is analytical and enquiring, and
those who are out to *recommend* something positive. The first
type stands back from humanity and asks, ' What is it? ' The
second type runs forward, pointing and beckoning the rest to
follow.

But this simple division, though useful as a preliminary, is really
an over-simplification, because every author combines both types,
the difference being in how the two are mixed. They all analyse
and investigate, and they all—even if they aren't fully conscious
of it—have something to recommend. The artist's function is
always to *humanize* the society he is living in, to assert the
importance of humanity in the teeth of whatever is currently
trying to annihilate that importance. In the Middle Ages, his task
was to assert the importance of humanity in the teeth of a religious orthodoxy, to declare that there could be and ought to be
such a thing as life here and now as well as life hereafter. Today,
the adversary is the machine; having surrounded ourselves with
mechanisms that are miracles of precision and refinement, we
have become so lost in contemplation of them that all our thinking has become mechanistic. Our ambition is to become machines
—then we shall be certain of the very best of everything. This
worship of the machine is a far worse tyranny than the Church,
even at its most megalomaniac, ever dreamed up; it is worse to
the precise degree that the television screen is more pervasive than
the pulpit, the loudspeaker louder than the human voice, the

aeroplane faster than the horse. This means that the job of humanizing our environment has to be taken more seriously than ever. *And he that is not with us is against us.*

But an author, whether he is going to preach to humanity or merely investigate it, has first to get himself into some intelligible relationship with the bulk of his fellow-creatures. Here is the first problem; let me indicate it with a quotation. It is always helpful to see how these things have been formulated by other people. Let us take that passage in Christopher Isherwood's *Lions and Shadows*, where the narrator goes to the seaside. He begins, you may remember, by indulging in a masochistic loathing-spree as he contemplates the English on holiday. At last, however, the reflection breaks in:

' But beneath all my note-taking, my would-be scientific detachment, my hatred, my disgust, there was the old sense of exclusion, the familiar grudging envy. For, however I might sneer, these people *were* evidently enjoying themselves in their own mysterious fashion, and why was it so mysterious to me? Weren't they of my own blood, my own caste? Why couldn't I—the would-be novelist, the professional observer—understand them? Why didn't I know—not coldly, from the outside, but intuitively, sympathetically, from within—what it was that made them perform their grave ritual of pleasure; putting on blazers and flannels in the morning, plus-fours or white trousers in the afternoon, dinner jackets in the evening; playing tennis, golf, bridge; dancing, without a smile, the foxtrot, the tango, the blues; smoking their pipes, reading the newspapers, organizing a sing-song, distributing prizes after a fancy-dress ball? True, I wasn't alone in my isolation. People like my friends and myself, I thought, are to be found in little groups in all the larger towns; we form a proudly self-sufficient, consciously declassed minority. We have our jokes, we amuse each other enormously; we are glad, we say, that we are different. But are we really glad? Does anybody ever feel sincerely pleased at the prospect of remaining in permanent opposition, a social misfit, for the rest of his life? I knew, at any rate, that I myself didn't. I wanted—however much I might try to persuade myself, in moments of arrogance, to the contrary—to find some place, no matter how humble, in the scheme of society. Until I do that, I told myself, my writing will never be any good; no amount of talent or technique will redeem it; it will remain a greenhouse product; something, at best, for the connoisseur and the clique.'

There we have the problem. And stating it in someone else's words is already a kind of comfort; it brings the sense that the difficulty is universal; if others have overcome it, it may be possible to learn from them how to succeed in one's turn; if they have all failed, one will either uniquely succeed, or fail in excellent company. There are many statements I might have quoted, but I chose Isherwood's because I find it, in tone and terms of reference, immensely sympathetic. Especially that bit about not wanting to be a greenhouse writer, admired by ' the connoisseur and the clique '. How one agrees! Better *no* reputation than the kind of reputation that accretes and clings to a Corvo, a Firbank, a Lautréamont even!

No, indeed, one doesn't want to stay in permanent opposition. But there is one thing worse—permanent conformity. No age in human history was ever so acceptable, so free of cankers and evils, that its more clear-sighted inhabitants could afford to string along with it *all* the time. A mechanical conformity, a mechanical rebelliousness, are both useless. The first has few temptations for an artist, the second many; especially as most artists are the type who fall easily into a pattern of unconventionality and defiance in childhood, and then tend to follow this pattern for sixty years after it has ceased to correspond to a genuine situation. How many an ageing genius, thundering defiance at the world, is in reality compensating himself for the mindless rigours of some loathsome little boarding-school back in 1912. On the other hand, the advice that is sometimes given to artists, that they should get on with their work and let society look after itself, is based on a lack of understanding of what their work *is*. What is needed, not just in artists, but in everyone who hopes to be more than a mere worker or mere drone in the hive, is a sense of touch. As I was making notes for this essay I heard a broadcast in which P. M. S. Blackett, the English scientist who is most widely accepted as spokesman for his calling, was being questioned about his views in general; several attempts were made to pin him down on the question of the scientific responsibility for extinction weapons; finally, asked point-blank whether or not a scientist was free to refuse to hand over the results of his research to irresponsible politicians and soldiers, he virtually threw up the whole subject in despair, with the words, 'No one is free, in a closely integrated society like ours.' This is certainly true, and an artist who claims to have *no* relationship with the society he lives in is claiming a freedom which he does not possess; even if he is a mystic, whose wants are limited to a prayer-mat and a begging bowl, it was probably some flaw in his relationship with society in general that drove him to adopt that position in the first place.

An artist, then, will have some position *vis-à-vis* the rest of the world whether he wants it or not—even if it is the sterile and undeveloping attitude of ' permanent opposition '—and his work, again whether he wishes it or not, will reflect his views on the matter. So it is in order for him to marshal his thoughts, from time to time, about what could broadly be called ' social ' issues. The chief danger is that he may be pushed too often into the rôle of social prophet. The public, at the moment, is in an alarmingly eager mood.

Signs are taken for wonders. ' We would see a sign !' The minute any kind of artist attracts attention, he is treated as a spokesman for his generation, his nation, his class, and what not. We have all seen, and deplored, the absurd results of the widespread journalistic habit of making *Lucky Jim* a symbol for anything that happened to be going about in search of a symbol. In all the mountains of print that have heaped up around that novel, there has been hardly a word of intelligent criticism. The overriding impulse, now more than ever, is to use any kind of articulate person—articulate with pen, with brush, with chisel, with musical notes—as a witch-doctor. The individual artist, who knows that his art is not merely another page of Hansard, is unwilling to have this rôle thrust on him; he veers away from it; so the solution is to find half a dozen or so who have some points of resemblance, then proclaim a Trend or a Movement. The latest of these fatuities is the Angry Young Man business; a phrase, I believe, originally applied to Mr Woodrow Wyatt, a politician, and subsequently extended far enough to include on the one hand a handful of poets, dramatists and novelists, and on the other such figures as Mr Colin Wilson and the late James Dean, both of whom belong to the active rather than contemplative life; they symbolize, in their own persons, the thing the others are supposed to be talking about. As a journalistic stunt, this will pass; the artist has merely to recognize, as one more fact about the world he is living in, that he has to be his own interpreter as well as the original provider of things to be interpreted; the journalists have abrogated their function; the task of comment, which in a better age he could have left to them, is now passed back to him again.

*   *   *

So one begins the process of trying to weigh up the society one is living in, and to find some coherent attitude towards it. And the first thing that stands out, to my mind, is the curious nature of the changes we are living through. Everyone always speaks of the twentieth century as an epoch of rapid change, so rapid as to be without parallel; old people, interviewed by the local press on their ninetieth birthdays, are always asked what changes they have seen, and always give the appropriate answer, the one that is expected of them; nothing, wherever they look, is what it was, or where it was, when they were young.

But when we look at this change in all its proliferation of detail, the most striking thing is not its extent, its completeness, but its lumpy and patchy quality. This lumpiness is observable both spatially (rapid change going on in one quarter, complete standstill in another) and temporally (curious stoppings and start-ings over a period of years). I find this most clearly illustrated when I consider the grown-ups' talk of 'the future' when I was a small boy. The generation of my parents had been brought up in a world that did not seem to them to be changing much (though I think they were wrong), and had, after 1914, been plunged into a mill-race of change from which they saw no prospect of ever emerging. They naturally assumed that every process of which they had seen the beginning would continue at the same pace. Take one detail: church attendance, for instance. Before 1914, if a tradesman wanted the custom of solid citizens, he had to turn up at church, and see to it that his family turned up with him; a doctor or solicitor who wanted to establish his practice couldn't afford to be known as a Freethinker; his place was at morning service with the rest of the respectable world. So the churches were always full. Then came the war, and a general untying of this kind of social corsetry; the churches attracted one in ten of their previous congregations, mostly older people. So, to my parents, it seemed natural to expect that when this remnant died off, nobody would go to church at all, and organized religion would be at a standstill. In fact, of course, the level has remained about where it was; all that had happened was that social pressure was relaxed, so that the only people who attended church were those who wanted to; if these were mainly the older people, that too was natural. In other words, an initial violent change was followed by a long period of stability. And this has happened in countless other spheres. Aviation, for instance. In 1930, when I was five, my elders took it for granted that in twenty years' time 'everyone would have his own aeroplane—like cars today.' For some years *Punch* had been publishing cartoons about traffic jams in the air, policemen on point-duty suspended from balloons, and so forth. And what happened? Long before I came of age, private aviation was as extinct as private charity.

In the field of politics it was the same. Most middle-aged people, when I was a boy, lived in continual expectation of a revolution, organized by 'the Reds'. (It was this fear of 'Reds', of course, that led our governing class to extend so warm a welcome to those sterling anti-Reds, Hitler and Mussolini, and thus involve us in the second war—and how easily we have forgiven them!) This fear was natural; they had seen 1916, both in Russia and, small-scale but near at hand, in Ireland; and they expected, once again, that the process, having started, would continue at about the same speed. Every strike, every hunger-march, was the work of the 'Reds', who were already hiding under the beds of old women of both sexes, ready to cut their throats. And here we are, nearly three decades further on, and the English working class have never been less Red in their history; all they are interested in is wringing higher and higher wages out of the bankrupt industries that employ them, with never a thought of altering the social structure in any way.

In fact, of course, what appeared to be the very rapid and sweeping changes brought about by the first world war had been well under way for some time. What the war did was to shake the fabric of ordinary convention so much that the new ideas were let loose. There was no longer any need to *épater le bourgeois*, because the bourgeois, in the pre-1914 sense of the word, no longer existed. So the immediate effect was that developments which had been carried on offstage, where the 'average man' couldn't see them, came on-stage. Very little was actually initiated in this period; in the arts, the real starting-point is in the years immediately before the shooting started. The 'new' literature of the twenties was mainly produced by men like Lawrence, Joyce, Wyndham Lewis, Pound and Eliot, who had got quite firmly started before the war. By contrast, a writer like Aldous Huxley, who was accepted by millions as a symbol of modernity, was only superficially an innovator. The ferment of ideas that many people associate with his work was in fact the *vulgarisation* of a process that had been going on, at the centres of discussion, for half a lifetime previously. Consider this sentence, describing the intellectual atmosphere at Oxford: 'There may have been too much restlessness and desire for change, there certainly was a tendency to treat everything as an open question, which led to a general sense of insecurity in matters of opinion.' When does that date from? The 1920's? No, the 1860's (*Life and Letters of Mandell Creighton*, 1913, chap. 3). And what is true of writing holds equally well for everything else. Mr David Sylvester, in a recent article (*Twentieth Century*, March 1957) has it this way:

' It seems to me that the twenty-five years or thereabouts leading up to the 1914 war were a time of astonishing creative ferment in almost every field. It was not only fine art that made a great leap of the imagination during this time. The foundations of modern logic and analytical philosophy were laid at this time by Frege, Russell and others, as were the foundations of psycho-analytic investigation by Freud and his colleagues. What has happened since in these fields might be just as aptly described as a specialized development of those initial discoveries as the art of the last forty years could be described as a specialized development of the discoveries of Cézanne and Monet and Gauguin and Rodin. And this even applies to the physical sciences. The invention or discovery of the aeroplane, of wireless telegraphy, of Röntgen rays, of the principles of atomic physics—these too belong to the time of Cézanne and early Picasso.'

With this tremendous leap, our century took off into space; and to people living in the twenties, it seemed that the changes must go on. In fact, I sometimes think that my generation, those who came of age immediately after the second war, were the first to grasp clearly that this was simply not happening. Where were all the things my parents and their friends used to prophesy when I was a nipper? Nowhere, it seemed, except in the pages of early Wells, mouldering on the shelves. Strangest of all was the attitude of people who had been young in the twenties, and were now getting into middle age. In their youth, it had seemed that the rigid crust of conventional life was cracking from top to bottom; a few more holes punched in it, and it would be nothing but a heap of crumbs. And behold! everything had somehow drifted back into something like the old shape; things like marriage, and private property, and war, and the division of the world into nations, and the Church, and the public schools—there they all were, the same as ever! To such people, the twentieth century must seem like one long tragic swindle. It isn't a new situation; an exactly parallel sequence of events happened in the lifetime of Wordsworth; he had just that glimpse of a new world, with

France standing on the top of golden hours,
And human nature seeming born again.

That's the trouble with new starts. Human nature is always seeming born again, and always growing up into much the same kind of shape as it always had.

Not that anyone of my age has had to face the problem of disillusionment. About the first fact we learnt about the world we were living in was that there aren't any new starts. From the age of ten, I inhabited a world in which everyone knew that a war was coming—i.e., that the War to End War had done nothing of the kind. The twenties had been an enormous gate, opening on to nothing special. One hardly knew whether to be glad or sorry that one hadn't been among the people who trooped through that gate, hearts beating high, and later had to adjust to the ordinariness of what they found. On the principle that to travel hopefully is better than to arrive, one should, I suppose, be sorry. Still, it can't be helped. What we have to cope with is this sense of being arrested in mid-air. Our whole society is suffering from a sensation very much like the one you get if you brace yourself to jump down ten stairs and then find it was only one. And this calls into being a special kind of intellectual nuisance: the crusading modernist, who is prepared to jump down ten stairs even if he has to dig a pit to do it. There he is, out of sight below ground-level in his pit, but his voice can be heard continually, making the same querulous demand to the rest of us to get our spades and do some digging.

In short, the position is difficult because of the slowness of change, not its speed. The surface of life has altered very quickly, but the inner core was re-structured in about 1912, and until the next major step forward—which may not be for a century or two, if ever—it is unlikely to alter much. Journalists don't realize this because they think that things like television, artificial satellites and cars with no clutches are signs of change—are, indeed, changes in themselves. But of course the only change worth taking any notice of is a change in character. If a man appears wearing a new suit, his baby daughter may think he has changed, but his wife and friends know that he hasn't.

This is what we have to get used to; this living with key ideas that are not new, that have already been absorbed—however incompletely—into the bloodstream of the community. Whenever we look up a date, we find ourselves staggered by the mere length of time all these ' modern ' ideas have been going. For instance, one of the last of the really ' basic ' books, the ones that put forward ideas which have since been accepted by *everyone*, was Freud's *Psychopathology of Everyday Life*. And Freud tells us in the preface that he established the basic idea in an essay, ' On the Psychic Mechanism of Forgetfulness', in 1898. In short, the whole thing is a nineteenth-century discovery; another instance, among thousands, of the fact that we are still living in the era created by those incredible frockcoated, bewhiskered giants.

In one way, the task of those of us who pick up the main burden now, in the fifties, is harder than it was for our predecessors. In the recent past, it was enough—or, at any rate, it was widely felt to be enough—if you were ' modern '; that is, if you welcomed the new ideas with a certain enthusiasm, and with whatever degree of misunderstanding and clumsiness. Auden's poems, with their hotch-potch mixing-in of every up-to-date idea, are the perfect document of ' modernism '; all the better as a document in that they have, after all, a certain quality that sets them apart from the merely rubbishy. As I say, you could get by. And you could also get by in the forties, without doing much more than be portentous and solemn. The war made genuinely constructive thought impossible, and at the same time created a demand for an acceptable substitute; as a result, the forties were the heyday of charlatanism. We are still plagued by some of the reputations that were first made in those slap-happy days, though the Great Healer is, I am happy to say, beginning to do his work.

But it is the present generation who are really brought face to face with these key ideas of our society; who can't, at this distance of time, get by on mere enthusiastic acceptance; who have to keep their heads.

*　　*　　*

What do I mean, in detail, by ' keeping our heads '? In the first place, a rejection of wholesale thinking and block attitudes. If a mechanical rebelliousness is futile, it is also true that an uncritical ' acceptance ' of the age one lives in is not so much culpable as impossible. How *can* anyone say that he accepts, or rejects, the twentieth century *en bloc*? It is too full of unresolved muddles for that. Not only have the forces of change acted patchily, leaving inert areas (e.g. the physical sciences have changed out of recognition, while the civil law has remained in the nineteenth century; we still cannot get rid of the death penalty or revolutionize the prison system); not only that, but the various eddies of modern thought have lost touch with one another. To take one example and let it stand for a thousand, consider our attitude to ' nature '; using the word, here, to mean the opposite of ' manmade' or 'artificial'. In one way, the twentieth century is great on Nature. The dominant science in our grandfathers' day was biology, and the metaphors on which they based all their thinking were derived from that study. Thus the metaphor of evolution coloured political and historical thinking and has survived unchanged in most academic disciplines till today. The dominant science of our time is psychology; it, too, has its leading metaphors, which have passed into popular thought, the most influential being the idea of repression and the uncovering of successive layers of consciousness, so that the layman's picture of the psychiatrist is of Peer Gynt contemplating his onion. And behind this lies the archetypal modern belief: it is unwise to tamper with Nature; the instinctual forces will go forward with a bull-like rush, and you must either stand out of the way or be gored. D. H. Lawrence, with his notion of the hidden springs of power, is the typical twentieth-century prophet; he saw this power as surging up from below the reach of the conscious mind, which could hamper but not command it. It is not too much to say that this belief, revolutionary when Lawrence first formulated it, has now taken unchallenged possession of the collective mind; virtually *everybody* agrees with it. So far, we are for Nature. And just as the mind must peel off its layers, so must the body. Let the sun shine for thirty minutes—even the watery sun of England—and every patch of grass is covered with nearly-naked figures, rapt, worshipping, mystically intent on soaking up the holy rays. *Nature*! Dive into the sea, roast in the sun, let your impulses grow up straight rather than tortuously—for grow they will, in some guise. Up to this point, it would seem that all of us, in our civilization, were unanimous in this at least. Until one looked round more widely.

Until one noticed, for instance, the kind of medical science we put our faith in. The chemists' shops, thronged all day with seekers after well-being—well-being in the shape of palliatives to ease symptoms; our medical laboratories where 'research' is directed to the frontal attack of these same symptoms. These places are reared and supported by the energy of an idea, and that idea is in flat contradiction of the worship of a beneficent Nature. Its theoretical basis is that Nature, too weak and faulty to defend

97

herself, is open to the assaults of hostile bacteria, which can only be combated by training a specially ferocious brand of antibiotics, like ferrets, to hunt them down. So the new wonder-drugs succeed each other at intervals of a few months; a new one is tried, it gobbles up the bacteria, the symptoms vanish, a victory is proclaimed in military metaphor ('such-and-such a disease is *conquered*'), and Nature is properly in her place. But of course, before the ink is dry on the newspapers that celebrate this victory, the evil bacteria have gone home and put on a new uniform, to reappear as something else—a new set of symptoms to be isolated and attacked. On with the job!—train a new cageful of ferrets! There's no nonsense here about Nature and her benevolence. If a man is ill, the answer is to pump him full of some chemical concoction whose job is to get in there and *work*. The same thing is seen in the now fashionable 'check-up'. Every few weeks one reads in the newspaper that some politician has gone into a nursing-home 'for a check-up'. If he is an American statesman, the findings will be made public; if an Englishman, they will be reticently concealed; but in either case the same thing has happened. A lung man has looked at his lungs, a liver man at his liver, a nose-and-throat man at his nose and throat, and so on. The more important he is, the more specialists he has. If he is as important as Mr Eisenhower, he can have a left knee-cap specialist to examine his left knee-cap, and a right knee-cap man for his right, if he wants to. These specialists have their own dynamic metaphor; they are detectives, and all the parts of the man's body are suspects, which have to be questioned, examined, weighed, and—if faulty—immediately chastised, i.e. set upon by the appropriate ferrets. Nature, in this context, is far from the numinously authoritative figure she assumes elsewhere. At worst she is an enemy, at best an erring child to be scolded and corrected.

Let this stand as an emblem of the difficulties of a man who wishes to reject, or accept, the age we live in. Here we have this hotch-potch of conflicting ideas about Nature; the distinguishing mark of the twentieth-century man, if he has one at all, is his willingness to hold these contradictory ideas simultaneously in his head. He trusts in Nature when he sun-bathes, or talks about the evils of 'repression' (thought of, in this connexion, as a kind of super-constipation); he mistrusts and fears her when he goes round to his doctor for a shot of penicillin. The confusion repeats itself in many other spheres; over materials, for instance. It is cheaper to make a thing out of plastics than out of wood or leather, so the more expensive craftsman makes a point of using natural materials, and 'artificial', in Elizabethan English a term of praise, comes to mean something cheap and nasty. Then we get the motor-car with its metal instrument panel painted to imitate the grain of wood. Lip-service to Nature, just as the electric light bulb set in a plastic imitation of a candle-stick is lip-service to age and primitive simplicity.

The word 'primitive', having at last cropped up, points to the area in which this confusion is a special concern of the artist. Primitivism, which is the artistic equivalent of sun-bathing and psycho-analysis, has dominated the arts for a long time now; the abandonment of metre and rhyme in poetry, which had set in by 1914, echoed the discovery, by visual artists, of the merits of rock-painting and native sculpture. But the drive towards the primitive was set in motion, and directed, by a sophisticated impulse to find new techniques to match the altered demands of the *Zeitgeist*—an impulse which was sufficient in itself to keep modern art at a wide remove from the *genuinely* primitive; in other words, the electric-light candle again, but this time as an artistic and intellectual necessity rather than a mere whim. (But the whim *derives* from the necessity; it corresponds to something real, after all.) In music, the technical discoveries of the previous three centuries were largely thrown away, and the new music repeated the blend of self-conscious technique and highly engineered 'freedom'. But I have said enough, for a topic which was introduced only as an example. How can one accept or reject? —the only course is to keep one's head.

This keeping one's head may seem too trivial to be erected into a serious ideal, but there are epochs in which it is the hardest thing one can do, and at the same time the most valuable. Historical parallels are misleading, and if I say that the present age seems to have some affinities with the period 1660-1700, I don't mean that we can use that or any other period as the basis for forecast. But that, like this, was a time of assessment and digestion; terribly destructive strife was a recent memory; clear thinking, rather than originality, was what counted. One fact that tends to confirm my belief in the accuracy of this assessment is the anger shown by many middle-aged people when they hear it. Some of the most scathing rejoinders that, as a critic, I have provoked, have been when, in no spirit of contention, I have remarked that the task of the immediate future seemed to me one of consolidation. On one such occasion, Mr Pritchett, amid much speculation about the cultural effects of free education and what-not, said sniffily that he 'could imagine a brighter future for literature'. So can I; I was not saying that my diagnosis was bright, merely that it was accurate. These people always assume that to say an era of experiment has ended is to imply that it has come to nothing. Whereas the problem of what to do with a mass of new material can be as urgent, and as challenging, as the problem of how to accumulate it in the first place.

According to my brief, I am supposed to say something, in this essay, about my own work and how it arises from the way I view things. The task is the simpler because so little of it has, at the moment of writing, been published, and not very much of that little has attracted any attention. My first novel, *Hurry on Down*, has been assimilated to the Angry Young Man business; my poems have been taken as evidence of the new literary conservatism and traditionalism; my criticism is supposed to show the new 'Redbrick' academicism, as opposed to the old fruity, porty academicism that has long been familiar. None of these assessments is anything but a caricature, though the caricature itself offers valuable evidence as to the nature of the group mind.[1]

---

[1] *For an ' assessment ' which neatly gathers all these strands into one, cf. Stephen Spender in Gemini, vol. 1, no. 1, p. 5: ' The undergraduates and instructors [sic] at the Redbrick Universities are fully aware of this [i.e. the ' urbanity ' of ' the senior universities '], and like to draw a distinction between their scholarship, their critical awareness, their intellectual intensity, and the Oxford-Cambridge softness and lack of any but genteel standards. Of course, this is a false dramatization. The real contrast today is between the Oxford-Cambridge assumption of collective superiority which to some extent atrophies the existence of each undergraduate and absorbs everything into its kind of classiness: and*

All artists who do not see themselves as mere entertainers are engaged in grappling with the problems that face the society they live in. And the artist cannot grapple with a problem, in his art, unless it is one that has got into his own life. He can indicate it, in an objective, critical way, by writing articles and so forth; but art is an affair of the whole man, and the whole man cannot respond to anything that has not been lived out. Hence 'Look in thy heart, and write' is still the primary adage, though it doesn't mean that all a writer has to do is gush and have 'sincerity', i.e. wear his heart on his sleeve. An artist can only have one principle: to treat whatever seems to him to present itself insistently for treatment, in the bit of life lived by him, in the corner of history and geography he inhabits. Thus, when I wrote *Hurry on Down*, the main problem which had presented itself in my own existence was the young man's problem of how to adapt himself to 'life', in the sense of an order external to himself, already there when he appeared on the scene, and not necessarily disposed to welcome him; the whole being complicated by the fact that in our civilization there is an unhealed split between the educational system and the assumptions that actually underlie daily life. We spend a good deal of money, both publicly and as individuals, on having the young taught to appreciate the masterpieces of literature and art; we maintain professors to lecture to them on philosophy and other high-flying subjects; and then we turn them out into a world that has no use for these things, a world whose operative maxim is 'Don't respect or consider anything except material powers and possessions.' The shock of this meeting is always a painful one, and the best work any teacher can do is to make it more painful, rather than cushion it. I myself had an exceptionally sheltered life, in this respect; I went straight from one university where I was learning to another where I was teaching; but this only exacerbated the sense of guilt I felt about the whole thing. So naturally I wrote a novel about a man who had been given the

---

the emphasis on squalor in writers like Kingsley Amis, John Wain, John Osborne, etc., which is the opposite side of the same medal of what is perhaps basically English class-consciousness.' I invite the reader to meditate on the style, as well as the substance, of this passage.

educational treatment and then pitchforked out into the world; adding for good measure, and for realism's sake, another cluster of problems which concerned the disappearance of the old-style *bourgeoisie*, among whom the hero was supposed to have been brought up. (He was widely taken by reviewers to be the typical scholarship boy, but that notion was derived not from the book, but from the surrounding air.) A top-dressing of emotional problems about women, and the thing was complete. When the mixture was stirred up and cooked, the central thing that emerged was a moral point—something to do with the nature of goodness—but nobody, except myself, saw this, so there is no point in bringing it up now. In outline, the book was quite conventional; its starting-point might have been that scene in *Antic Hay* where Gumbril, having thrown up his job as a schoolmaster, comes home and confronts his father.

"Well, well," said Gumbril Senior, sitting down again, "I must say I'm not surprised. I'm only surprised that you stood it, not being a born pedagogue, for as long as you did. What ever induced you to think of turning usher I can't imagine."
. . . "What else was there for me to do?" asked Gumbril Junior, pulling up a chair towards the fire. "You gave me a pedagogue's education and washed your hands of me."

Thirty years separate *Antic Hay* and *Hurry on Down*, but the situation of the young man has not changed; he must still set out from that starting-point: 'You gave me a pedagogue's education and washed your hands of me.' Because *any* liberal education, in the world we have moved into, is 'a pedagogue's education'; its only direct application must be in perpetuating itself, by handing the same material on to another generation. It cannot turn outwards into the world at large, because the world rejects it. This, in short, was the situation that had met me in my own life, and accordingly this was what I wrote about. I followed it up with a novel that was meant to be constructive, and to attack fashionable despair and nihilism; the man decides to commit suicide on the first page, and on the last he looks back and wonders how he could have been so misguided; life intervenes and teaches him the necessary lessons. The failure of this book was so spectacular that

I can only assume that everyone found it literally unreadable; certainly very few of the comments it received were any use to me, because they all seemed to be by people who had not read further than the first ten pages: e.g. one journalist quite recently attacked the book as 'hysterical', because it gave a picture of contemporary young manhood as seedy, despairing, self-lacerating, etc.: he should have made it clear that he was taking the first chapter and letting it stand for the whole, a procedure which, if generally adopted, would revolutionize criticism. There is nothing one can do about this, except admit that the book failed to reach an audience, and write it off.

With regard to the future, all I can do is to go on trying to tackle the problems of contemporary life as they confront me personally: 'tackle' them by seeking to give them adequate literary expression, rather than 'solve' them. A writer makes his books out of his ignorance and folly, as much as out of his knowledge and wisdom; *King Lear* is as much about what Shakespeare didn't know as about what he did—and all the more human for that. As far as novels are concerned, I suppose I shall try to grasp these problems in clusters, rather than singly. Problems don't occur in isolation, they occur in the context of other problems. For instance, I have completed a novel (*The Contenders*), to be published in 1958, which tries to tackle the problem of (a) material ambition as a corrupting power, (b) rivalry as ditto, (c) whether personal relationships or 'work' in the Carlylean sense is the better foundation for a life, (d) the metropolitan versus the provincial virtues, i.e. 'being in touch' versus 'sturdy independence'. I have tried not to write the book as an arid thesis, but to allow all these issues to spring naturally from the interplay of theme and character and to attract towards themselves any other issues which may be thrown up *en route*. The novel is a useful form for this kind of treatment because it lends itself to the slow unfolding of a cluster of themes; it gives both writer and reader time to turn round in; Lawrence meant something of this kind, I suppose, when he said that if *Hamlet* had been a novel it wouldn't have been so mysterious. More clarification in detail could have been provided. Other forms, notably poetry, strike me as useful in dealing with emotional and moral problems at the point of crisis.

The kind of short, compressed poem that I write, at any rate, is meant to present its subject-matter with the immediacy of the sudden shocks you get in life. The short story, too, can work in something like the same way by picking the moment when a thing comes to the boil and relying on suggestion to convey what lies before and after. However, there are many kinds of poem and story, and I don't want to sound unwilling to try, at any time, something quite different from what I have sketched here. At any rate, the basic equipment of any artist is (i) an interest in the technical details of his art, (ii) a willingness to respond to the life about him—what Dr Leavis calls 'a reverent openness to experience '; and this twofold equipment I hope and believe that I have; the rest is largely a matter of luck.

Having spoken of 'luck', I must put in a qualification, otherwise I shall have the straw-in-the-hair, manna-from-heaven brigade thinking I am coming round to their side. In the arts (as, perhaps, in life?) 'luck' comes to those who put themselves in the way of it; the bird of inspiration will perch on your shoulder all the more readily if your shoulder is dusted and held in the most favourable position. That is the importance of (i) above: an interest in the technical side of one's art. You can't love the soul of literature without loving her body. At the moment of writing (though this may not apply when this comes to be printed), the technical problem most insistently present to my mind is that of tragi-comedy. In my first two novels, I made a fairly rough-and-ready attempt at the presentation of serious issues through the medium of very broad comedy, not to say outright farce. There was no attempt at delicate shading from one mood to another; on the contrary, it was the violent juxtaposition that made the effect, as far as I was concerned. The justification of this method, I thought, was its realism; 'life' is, notoriously, like that, always mingling the grotesquely comic with the sombre or even tragic. I am not sorry I made these two attempts, but in future I want to achieve more of a compound, rather than a mixture, of elements; I still think that the novel, to get in a wide enough sweep of life, needs comic as well as sombre ingredients, but I find myself increasingly inclined to doubt whether art can afford to imitate life as directly as that; because our raw experience comes to us in unsorted lots, doesn't mean that when we come to interpret it imaginatively we should still keep it in the same jumble. Of course the need for tragi-comedy has always been recognized; you could extract a good enough working programme from Dr Johnson's words:

'Shakespeare's plays are not in the rigorous and critical sense either tragedies or comedies, but compositions of a distinct kind; exhibiting the real state of sublunary nature, which partakes of good and evil, joy and sorrow, mingled with endless variety of proportion and innumerable modes of combination; and expressing the course of the world, in which the loss of one is the gain of another; in which, at the same time, the reveller is hasting to his wine, and the mourner burying his friend; in which the malignity of one is sometimes defeated by the frolick of another; and many mischiefs and many benefits are done and hindered without design.'

I cannot think of any resounding peroration, to finish with; but I do know that the best hope for a significant and valuable literature is that those who have chosen writing as a profession should *do their best*—should think of their work as serious, and not be afraid to seem in earnest about it. One of the plagues of modern life is that a literary man has a certain status; it is worth the trouble to acquire a reputation as a writer if your aims are social or even pecuniary; such a reputation can be used as an instrument in the furthering of all sorts of ambitions which have nothing to do with literature, nothing to do with the state of our civilization, nothing to do with anything except the writer's own personal advancement. At the moment, the literary world is organized very conveniently for such people; the smart magazines, which should be playing an important part in the dissemination of ideas, are too often used simply as a stage on which the latest candidate for public attention can display his bag of tricks. The trouble with this is not merely that people become materially successful who don't deserve to; that doesn't matter, and will in any case always happen; 'getting on' isn't important. The danger is that when *every* book is reviewed by some charlatan whose only concern is to leave the reader with an impression of *his* cleverness, *his* personality, *his* graceful style, when *every* magazine is edited by someone whose object is to keep intact the network of social and political relationships that permitted his own rise to power, in short, when every genuine object is submerged in a general grabbing for plums and security—then the intellectual life of the country will be at a standstill. The only hope is that people—ordinary, non-writing people—will not stand for it; that the *flâneur* who tries to get by on 'style' and 'wit' will be sharply challenged to produce his credentials; that the critic who never risks a personal judgement, but merely hands on the valuations that are current in his circle, will be needled into speaking for himself once in a while. And perhaps finally—but this, I admit, is Utopian —it will become conventional to measure a man's worth by his solid achievement instead of his slickness and showmanship.

All this matters because civilized life depends on a certain amount of discrimination, which provides the climate in which excellence can be seen and encouraged. And this is what a man of creative talent has the right to demand of the society he lives in; it is a *right*, not a luxury. Imaginative work is difficult, exhausting, always lonely and frequently agonizing; I do not see how any society can have the face to ask an artist to undergo the ordeal of creation unless it is prepared to meet him half-way by making the effort of discrimination. That is why I have so hammered this point about keeping one's head, about having balance and critical awareness. The present phase of history finds Western mankind in the position of an inexpert tightrope walker, who has launched himself with a slithering rush, and now finds himself halted, with a sea of upturned faces below him, and the second half of his journey to go. *That* is why we cannot afford charlatanism; it is also why the young must continue to ignore their elders who jeer at them for being cautious, for dealing in half-measures, for not having 'passion' or being 'committed'. Some of my generation have fallen for this claptrap and taken in their turn to advocating a blind rush along the rest of the tightrope. I believe we must have the nerve to go on step by step; and that means having the courage to say No to our fools, however influential and important they may be.

Theatre
and living

KENNETH TYNAN

Kenneth Tynan

Born in Birmingham, 1927. Won demyship to Magdalen College, Oxford. Was President of the Experimental Theatre Club, Editor of the *Cherwell*, and Secretary of the Oxford Union. 1949: appointed director of weekly repertory company in Lichfield, Staffordshire; six months directing. First book published, collection of general and particular opinions about the theatre called *He That Plays the King*, with preface by Orson Welles. 1952: appointed drama critic of the *Evening Standard*. 1953: two more books published—*Persona Grata*, pen portraits of a hundred of his favourite living people, with photographs by Cecil Beaton, and *Alec Guinness*. Row with *Evening Standard*, and joined *Daily Sketch* as drama critic. 1954: succeeded Ivor Brown as drama critic of the *Observer*. Meeting Brecht and subsequent experience of the Berliner Ensemble in 1955 and 1956 confirmed his admiration of a man he had first begun to study in 1949. In 1956 a fourth book *Bull Fever*—personal views on bull-fighting and the allied art of drama. First radio play, Third Programme extravaganza, called *The Quest for Corbett*, written in collaboration with Harold Lang. Joined Ealing Studios as script editor, acting in advisory capacity to Sir Michael Balcon. 1957: first film script adapted from novel *Nowhere to Go* and written in collaboration with Seth Holt. Work in progress on a book about his last ten years' experience and how it has changed his whole attitude to drama. Plans for the future: 'More work in films, more drama criticism and perhaps, if I can forget for a few months how insuperably difficult it is to write one, a play.'

FROM definitions everything follows, so with a definition I shall begin this ragbag of an aesthetic credo in which, very probably, aesthetics will not be mentioned at all. Good drama, for me, is made up of the thoughts, the words and the gestures that are wrung from human beings on their way to or in or emerging from a state of desperation. A play is an ordered sequence of events that brings one or more of the people in it to a desperate condition, which it must always explain and should if possible resolve. If the worst that can happen is the hero's being sent down from Oxford, we laugh and the play is a farce; if death is a possibility, we are getting close to tragedy. Where there is no desperation, or where the desperation is inadequately motivated, there is no drama; characters, for instance, who scream when their noses are tickled or commit suicide the day after falling in love are bad cases of inadequately motivated desperation. These broad rules apply not only to all successful drama from Aristophanes to Beckett, but also to the other narrative arts of novel and film.

Drama varies from age to age, nowadays almost from week to week, because every age has a new threshold of desperation, a new definition of the pressures that cause it. In antiquity, a bad omen from the soothsayer would have been enough. More recently, a sour look from the monarch. More recently still, excommunication. And plays are even now being written in which social ostracism, rejection by 'The Establishment', is presented as an adequate reason for human despair. All these motives are as dead as the societies that created them. Yet, in British drama at least, they won't lie down; and plays continue to be written on the assumption that there are still people who live in awe of the Crown, the Empire, the established Church, the public schools and upper classes. Meanwhile the really big, belligerent, international problems—poverty, ignorance, oppression and the rest —are theatrically shunned. The mansion of drama is cluttered with debris, ancient assumptions that Shaw bashed and cracked but failed to dislodge. The job of new playwrights is to remove the rubble, to sweep the floor; to make room, in a theatre which is, as Arthur Miller said, ' hermetically sealed off from life ', for the real causes of contemporary human pain. This means that a number of simple platitudes must be reasserted, platitudes about equality of chance, abolition of want, rejection of life after death in favour of life on earth; old stuff, of course, too yawn-provoking, but if we want a responsible drama we must go on plugging it, even though it evokes shrieks of boredom from people intelligent enough to know better. A sensation was lately caused in Russia by Dudintsev's novel entitled *Not by Bread Alone*. Our theatre needs a similar sensation, though the name of the play that might create it would be different. It would be called: *Not by Cake Alone*.

' We've heard it all before ' is the cult cry whenever a play ' gets social '. Of course we have: but we have not acted on the advice. Our stages are still overgrown with petty snobberies and glib acceptances; and we still judge plays as if a critic needed no other attributes than an ear for a well-turned phrase, an eye for a good performance and an entire absence of convictions. Since the squibs of Shaw and the sprawling Galsworthy epics, this country has produced almost no sociological drama; and I am using ' sociological ' in the widest sense, the sense in which it applies to Shakespeare's twin summits, the two parts of *Henry IV*. There must, one feels, be something profoundly wrong with a theatre that boasts, in Sir Laurence Olivier, the best actor alive, yet can tempt him into modern dress only once in twenty years. Good technical playwrights abound, but among them no great questioner, no one who might uproot our deepest assumptions and turn the full glare of his mind on them; no one who could explain why we still stand for the national anthem, while imaginary generals pin imaginary medals to our breasts; no one who could show us how odd it is that we should be surprised to find a dustman sitting beside us at a performance of a first-rate play; no one, in short, who can dramatize what we feel about our world. There are so many questions that our drama has scarcely begun to formulate, far less to answer. Can social changes remove the sources of desperation? Why, even in a world of peace and full employment, might a human being still try to kill himself? Of Marx and Freud, which is the chicken and which the egg? If you feel that these things are none of the theatre's business, you had better retire to your ivory tower and softly, softly turn the key. A drama of 'no comment' is a drama of no future. Art of any kind that turns its back on the world is uncivilized in the precise and single sense of the word.

Three attitudes towards life are open to the dramatist. He can mirror it, in sickness and in health, on the principle that art imitates life. He can seek to change it, on the equally valid principle that life imitates art. Or he can withdraw from it into a private fantasy, connected with the objective world only peripherally and by chance. This is the trickiest way of all, and for every sane writer who takes it there are a dozen paranoiacs. Withdrawal from mundane life is a fitting course for some poets and all mystics, not to mention those serene and exceptional human beings who follow the precepts of Zen Buddhism; but it seldom works in a place as social and public as a theatre. The sort of temperament that prefers to steer clear of reality had better steer clear of the drama, unless of course it belongs to a towering genius; for at the end of that line lies solipsism, and the belief, not uncommon in certain Parisian circles, that communication between human beings is not so much difficult as impossible; and even, in the last resort, undesirable. I don't know what you think of extremists like that. They remind me of people who habitually wear strait-jackets and then blame the world for the virtual impossibility of shaking hands. Or they put me in mind of Houdini, and the legend that tells of his single defeat: how he failed, after hours of effort, to escape from a prison cell, the door of which (he afterwards learned) had never been locked.

Dramatists who want to change the world seldom write very subtly, and there is no reason why they should. Subtlety operates best in a *status quo*, just as ripples are best seen in a standing pool. In a stormy sea only waves are visible; and we, who live in imminent danger of the hydrogen tempest, need plays that are waves, and big, crashing ones at that. There will be time later for what is exquisite, what is filigree; for the blander locutions that come of security. If all art is a gesture against death, it must not stand by while Cypriots are hanged and Hungarians machine-gunned, and the greater holocaust prepares. It must go on record; it must commit itself. I want drama to be vocal in protest; and I frankly do not see whence the voices will come if not from the Left.

The young Leftists who have emerged in Britain since the war are a flourishing bunch, worth more than a passing word. They are different from the radical intelligentsia of the thirties in one vital respect: they are not engaged in filial revolt against the class from which they sprang. For the most part they are state-educated lower-middles, and they regard the country-house class neither with envy nor with disdain, but with sheer, laconic boredom. Their attitude towards palace-dwellers is much the same. They are fully aware that small nations tend to venerate what is peculiar to them. Spain has its bullfights; San Marino its postage-stamps; Britain its queen. But things are getting wildly out of hand when a popular columnist can quote with passionate endorsement an Australian soldier's description of the Queen, the Duke and their children as 'just about the four most important people in the world'. The Left exists to combat such ludicrous excesses, and that is just what its younger adherents are doing: recalling writers to the writer's basic job, which is never to lose sight of the ways in which ordinary people think and feel and eat and earn and work. The playwright's audience is his raw material, and he has a double duty towards it: not only to enliven and enlighten it, but to concern himself with the social environment that makes it what it is.

At this point some kind of political commitment becomes inevitable. If an audience is cocooned in prejudice and apathy, to influence it from the stage is not enough; one must work, if one is a whole man, for a society less prejudiced, less apathetic. To write plays for the national theatre is no use unless one is an active supporter of the party that promises to build a national theatre. If playgoers are narrow-minded, one must take part in the process of broadening their minds; which means reforming the educational system so that its approach to history and culture is not national but international, and insular only in so far as the world is a spherical island in space. Art that cares nothing for these things is a thinking flower that conspires at its own death by ignoring the soil in which it grows. As long as it does not impair his vision, or exclude from his work the virtues of pity and irony, a political belief is the most enriching thing that can happen to a writer.

I don't mean, of course, that style is unimportant; nor that I could admire a shoddily-written play merely because I agreed with its content. In all the arts, what is being said is always modified and often invalidated by the way in which it is said. I get a brisk daily reminder of this from my four-year-old daughter. Every morning, at her urgent request, I tell her the story of the play I saw, as a critic, the night before. I rapidly discovered that it mattered very little to her what the characters did, or how they felt. I would try to describe the fearful plight of X, or the ghastly suffering of Y, but always my daughter would break in with the simple, succinct question: ' Yes, but *what did he say?* ' What interested her were the exact words, the precise reaction to events. There is no other word for that but style.

On the other hand, I could never cheer a play, no matter how well-written, the content of which I found wholly offensive. If Belloc had written a play defending anti-Semitism, or if Evelyn Waugh were to write a play extolling hereditary aristocracy, I should be instinctively hostile; and I should be far more lenient towards a crude writer who cared about total human survival. Once, to explain the difference between the drama of the past and the drama of the future, Bert Brecht cited a news picture he had seen of the Tokyo earthquake. Everything was razed and devastated, except for a few modern buildings. The caption read: ' Steel stood.' ' If you compare that,' said Brecht, ' with the elder Pliny's description of the eruption of Etna, you will see what I mean.' Pliny was an accomplished writer: but he failed to achieve, in thousands of words, what the caption achieved in two: it told us how to survive. All art that doesn't try to do just that—and a great clown, I might add, can do it with a gesture— is finally frivolous. To quote Brecht again: the only questions worth asking nowadays are those that can be answered.

Writing about popular art and its effect on working people, Richard Hoggart said a strong thing: 'Whilst they are enjoying it, people may submit themselves, may identify themselves; but at the back of their minds they know it is not "real"; "real" life goes on elsewhere. Art may "tek yer *out* of yourself"; but the form of that phrase indicates that there is, inside, a "real" you for which art is not expected to speak; except to reflect, by conventional means, certain agreed assumptions.' Whenever the theatre encourages the idea of art as an irrelevant distraction, as it usually does, it becomes socially damnable; for it thereby sustains the myth that 'real' art, 'real' culture, is minority culture, intended for the few and best left to them. According to this fiction, all artists are outsiders; which leads to the even more pernicious corollary, that all outsiders are artists. To believe that unusual or inflammatory plays belong only to a minority is a confession of despair, and it is because I cannot subscribe to it that I cannot bring myself to mourn the decimation undergone in recent years by the little club theatres of London. The very existence of private theatres tends to corroborate the notion that art is produced by and for an egghead Mafia of crazy individualists, all busy affirming their separateness from the world; arty-crafty lot they are, let them get on with it, don't waste your money. A private theatre is in fact an excrescence created by the laziness of public theatres and the myopia of censorship. A rash of club theatres is tangible evidence that the commercial theatre is sick and falling down on its job. They are places where ideas that might surprise and instruct the many are presented to the few who are already familiar with them: thus the law ensures that *avant-garde* drama preaches only to the converted.

There are no club theatres in Paris or New York, because in neither city is there an official censor. There are none in Berlin, because in that wide-open frontier post experimental plays are instantly incorporated into the repertoires of the large subsidized theatres. Ideally, plays 'for members only' should be available to everyone. But in London this would only be possible if the Lord Chamberlain were abolished, if state aid were increased, and if the laws relating to Sunday opening of theatres were revised. Here again we find that politics and theatre are indivisible. It is good to have fine plays and fine actors to perform them, just as it is good to have fine cars and fine drivers to steer them. But one also needs petrol, a garage and an open road.

*   *   *

All of us owe a great debt to semantic philosophy for having taught us to talk sense, and to distinguish always between empirical, analytic, metaphysical, attitude and value statements. We have been trained to verify what we say, and we know that statements in the last three categories cannot be verified at all. So far, so good: we are less deceived than we used to be. But who are we? Intellectuals, presumably. And here lies the snag. The new philosophy has taught us to eschew moral affirmatives and the use of 'ought', but it has made no impact at all on the great mass of people, who are still as enslaved to vague rhetorical statements as ever they were. We can prove that these statements are meaningless, but we are forbidden to replace them with social exhortations (attitude-statements) or proposals for a better life on earth (value-statements). The resulting spectacle is not so much of the blind leading the blind as of the gelded leading the drugged. We have artists afraid to affirm anything addressing an audience that believes either nothing or nonsense. When that kind of deadlock is reached, it is time for the heart to take over from the head.

In the spring of 1957, a public-opinion poll revealed that seventy-one per cent of the adult population of Britain believed Jesus Christ to be the son of God. Not just a magnificent human being, but the direct offspring of the deity. Now I believe that one of art's abiding tasks is to restore the balance when the scales of popular thinking have tipped too far in one direction. If the poll was correct, unreason had clearly been tipping the scales for a very long time; yet, apart from Nigel Dennis's *The Making of Moo*, there are no openly atheistic plays in the English repertory. Most educated people are agreed in denying the divinity of Christ; yet nowhere is their opinion reflected in the theatre. And I think I know why. Most playwrights belong to the unbelieving twenty-nine per cent: and they are fully aware that if they question Christ's godhead their sharpest opponents will be drawn not from the believing majority but from their own fellow-agnostics, who will instantly deride them for being old-fashioned. And that, the cruellest cut, brings us back to: 'We've heard it all before.' We have, indeed, in novels and essays and works of philosophy; but not (and this is the crux of the matter) in the theatre. Similarly, the ideas articulated by Jimmy Porter in John Osborne's *Look Back in Anger* were not, by average intellectual standards, new: but they were explosively new in the theatre. We must destroy the idea that drama is always fifty years behind the times, even if it means running the gauntlet of our intelligent friends to do it.

I have mentioned metaphysics; and this may be the moment to deal with a group of young writers who have recently made a determined attempt to capture the believing majority in the name of 'a new religion' and 'a spiritual revival'. To people already conditioned by such uplift sedatives as *The Power of Positive Thinking*, by Norman Vincent Peale, they have offered the added incitement of intellectual arrogance. One must be impatient with these young *Führers* of the soul, fantasy-Leopolds and fantasy-Loebs, who declare that Hitler, for all his faults, was after all an outsider, and who commit themselves to stating that 'the most irritating of the human lice is the humanist with his puffed-up pride in reason.' One touch of Nietzsche, as someone said, makes the whole world kin. But perhaps I am taking these striplings too seriously. Some of them, after all, have barely started Shavian.

Religion, described by Remy de Gourmont as a machine for creating remorse, inevitably leads us to sex, which is as various in its forms as the clothes and the ears and the legs and the hair and the breasts and the postures that coalesce into male or female excitement. Yet the theatre, whenever sex in any form is on the agenda, dissolves into squirming inhibitions, anguished titters, nervous outbursts and defiant hypocrisy; all the masks behind which sexual guilt is most readily concealed. Anything that would help to divorce sex from guilt in the minds of audiences and playwrights alike would make for a healthier drama; and the first condition for this is the stringent undermining of institutions that uphold the idea of original sin. The prime enemy is Pauline Christianity, with its horrified distaste for the sexual act and its quietly disgusted tolerance of men who cannot resist their baser appetites and had therefore better marry than be damned. Shaw's words still hold true: 'There has really never been a more monstrous imposition perpetrated than the imposition of the limitations of Paul's soul upon the soul of Jesus.' Men who swallow Paul's dogmas make that worst of all kinds of marriage, wherein contempt at length breeds familiarity. The fullest indictment of Christian misogyny has been made by Simone de Beauvoir: 'Fear of the other sex,' she says, 'is one of the forms assumed by the anguish of man's uneasy conscience,' and she aptly cites Tertullian's definition of woman as ' a temple built over a sewer ', coupled with Augustine's assertion that procreation is always sinful, because of ' the obscene commingling of the sexual and excretory organs '. Monasticism, the horrified male protest, is best exposed by Gibbon's translation of a fifth-century comment on the monks of Capri: ' How absurd is their choice! how perverse their understanding! to dread the evils, without being able to support the blessings, of the human condition. Either this melancholy madness is the effect of disease, or else the consciousness of guilt urges these unhappy men to exercise on their own bodies the tortures which are inflicted on fugitive slaves by the hand of justice.' The taboos that govern our sexual lives, and hence the theatrical presentation of them, are idiotically *démodés*. One feels like a man with a speedboat who is trying to cut through a network of canals that are choked with weeds and blocked with locks. How one longs for a play which might remind us that what truly differentiates us from the animals is merely that we *know* we are the same!

If human history is the chronicle of man's efforts to overcome his sense of separation from the rest of mankind, the only valid religion is that which helps history to fulfil itself. I know love, as a word, is laughable, but it remains the only way: not the neurotic kind of love, whereby a man spends his life seeking a partner with a wound that matches his teeth: nor the surrendering kind that sends the over-mothered man flying to the maternal woman, and the over-fathered girl to the paternal man: nor yet what the French call *égoïsme à deux*, where two frightened lovers build a protective wall to keep out the hostile world. I am talking about the key dogma, which is self-love. ' If you love yourself,' said Meister Eckhart, ' you love everybody else as you do yourself.' This does not mean selfishness; rather the opposite, for the selfish man usually despises and mistrusts himself. 'Love thy neighbour as thyself' is a maxim stated the wrong way round: you must love yourself first. Otherwise you fall into the sickness of Strindberg's hero in *The Road to Damascus*, who said that he would like to obey the commandment, only he knew that if he did so he would end by 'hating my neighbour as much as I hate myself'. To know yourself is the first step. To love what you know is the second. To love others as much is the third. To love one other person is the fourth and last. So ends the lesson, and we had better get back to the theatre.

Somewhere in *Les Mandarins*, Mme de Beauvoir says that the aim of the artist should be to write something that might keep an intelligent young man up all night. This means drama with a world-view behind it. First decide what you think of 'that horrid old bore, the human predicament' (I quote from a B.B.C. radio talk), and then make a play of it. Don't begin by trying to exploit either the architecture or the conventions of theatre as it exists, since neither were created with such ambitious projects in mind. If the world is transformable—and that, according to Brecht, is what every writer must believe—then the theatre is transformable as well.

What kind of world view do I most enjoy in the theatre? I have dropped a few hints already, most of them fairly clangorous. I want plays that are Brechtian in their internationalism, their loathing of hero-worship, their mordant rejection of verbal frills (leave them to bourgeois-decadent critics like myself, don't festoon human lips with their foolery), and their conviction that 'to talk of trees is almost a crime, since it implies silence about so many enormities.' I want plays that affirm candour, valour, grace and sensuality; and plays that recoil from determinism, because determinism denies free choice, and without free choice there can be no drama. As Samuel Beckett's *Fin de Partie* showed, the play that is bound to a mechanistic universe is also bound to despair: when protest is absent, the step from 'this is how life is' to 'this is how life should be' is frighteningly short.

I prefer enthusiasms; not necessarily on the surface, as in writers like Tennessee Williams or the Australian Ray Lawler, but concealed as well, as a thermos flask may contain great heat without radiating it. Fear of ebullience is a great enemy of our culture : it freezes the pipes. It crops up in the most disconcerting places, as when an *Observer* correspondent reported how a group of Chinese university students had told him, 'with somewhat chilling enthusiasm', that they were busy making a new world. 'Somewhat chilling': the phrase is full of frigid distaste: one sees horns hastily pulled in, contacts rapidly avoided, with more than a flicker of disdain.

But there are malevolent enthusiasms as well, generated by our society at its worst, and these I wish the drama would take pains to quell. A few months ago, in one of Lord Beaverbrook's papers, a series of articles appeared on the general topic of 'How to Make a Million'. The last of them revealed, with rare and appalling nudity, the values on which our world is based. Let me quote from the author's 'rules for success':

'BE TOUGH. Be so tough that sentiment has no place in your life. Be so tough that if your dearest friend stands in the way of a business deal you can sweep him aside.

BE AMBITIOUS. Be so ambitious that it becomes an overriding consideration in your life. Smash your way onwards as if everyone was your foe, to be trampled on in the jungle of commerce. And preferably wear hobnailed boots for the job. . . .

DEVELOP A TRADING SENSE. Seize the bargains before the other man can get them. If he complains that you took advantage of his simplicity, ignore his complaints and damn the consequences.

APPLY YOUR MIND TO YOUR JOB. . . . Think day and night about money making. Live with it, dream about it, talk about it . . . you should be utterly devoted to one aim, and utterly ruthless in its prosecution.'

In all this there is no ironic intention : it is a serious statement of faith. It is called, I believe, rugged realism; and, by all that's human, it will have to go. After reading such an untender manifesto, my mind goes back to what used to be a fundamental Christian premise: that usury is evil *per se*, since the most unnatural of all practices is that by which money is made to breed money. That was Shylock's error, as the play makes clear: he cannot understand why dead metal should not bring forth of its own kind, he can see no difference between gold and silver on the one hand, and ewes and rams on the other. Yet where, since Shakespeare, is an English play that condemns the lifeless procreation of currency? I do not think it exists.

*   *   *

The trouble with most Socialist drama, and with much Socialist thinking, is its joylessness. We think of social plays in terms of anger, squalor, dourness and violence. In part, that is unavoidable, because plays of protest are meant to shock people into action by the brute presentation of fact. But there is room, none the less, for more left-wing satire of the kind that bubbled so hotly in Sartre's play *Nekrassov*, which pinked its opponents instead of pounding them to death. A peevish stridency overcomes, all too often, the Socialist wit; a cawing note distorts his laughter; and one begins to suspect, as the Tories are ever eager to point out, that his politics are merely a projection of an unresolved psychological conflict. Socialism ought to mean more than progress for its own sake: it ought to mean progress towards pleasure. And this is where one runs up against the impenetrable frown of the nonconformist conscience. The true statement—'The Tories are wicked, and have most of the fun '—gets perverted into : ' The Tories are wicked, *because* they have most of the fun.' Puritanism has won the match; and fun, in the theatre at least, has become very nearly a Tory monopoly. Left-wing humour seldom reaches the stage without declining into a prim Orwellian sourness. Ever since the Restoration, the English image of a wit has been an imperturbable *flâneur* who would never stoop to the vulgarity of meaning what he says; to this image even Shaw conformed, and Tory audiences laughed without discomfiture, being perfectly sure that he did not intend to be taken seriously. Nor was he, nor is he, so taken; and we are still deficient in plays that are socially critical at the same time as they are uproariously funny. We miss the sound of *responsible* gaiety. And we could do with more of those detonating farces that are written by anarchists, who are usually Socialists driven to drink by the anti-fun bias of English Socialism.

To discover that one is a Socialist should be a liberating experience. The obvious comparison is with the early Protestants. What did it feel like (and I shall quote at length from C. S. Lewis's monumental *English Literature in the Sixteenth Century*) to be one of them?

'One thing is certain. It felt very unlike being a 'purian' such as we meet in nineteenth-century fiction. Dickens' Mrs Clennam, trying to expiate her early sin by a long life of voluntary gloom, was doing exactly what the first Protestants would have forbidden her to do. They would have thought her whole conception of expiation papistical.'

And later:

'The experience is that of catastrophic conversion. The man who has passed through it feels like one who has woken from nightmare into ecstasy. Like an accepted lover, he feels that he has done nothing, and never could have done anything, to deserve such astonishing happiness.'

He has, so to speak, jumped the queue, found the direct pipeline to God, realized that to be alive is to be in a state of bliss; for him there is no need of hierarchies, and he cannot see why intermediaries should be appointed to interpret God's will to him.

' He is not saved because he does works of love: he does works of love because he is saved. . . . From this buoyant humility, this farewell to the self with all its good resolutions, anxiety, scruples and motive-scratchings, all the Protestant doctrines originally sprang.'

They were doctrines 'not of terror, but of joy and hope'. Where the Papists extolled virginity, the Protestants exalted marriage. And Dr Lewis brilliantly demonstrates how far they were from what we call puritanism. 'Whatever they were, they were not sour, gloomy or severe; nor did their enemies bring any such charge against them.' Thomas More upbraided them for their 'lewd lightness of minde and vayne gladnesse of harte', and said that Luther had made converts because 'he spiced al the poison' with 'libertee'. Even Calvin, whose insistence on sexual discipline was quite as strict as that of Rome, emphatically approved of 'delight and merriment' in food, and bravery of apparel. In early Protestantism we hear none of the self-denying falsehoods with which Catholicism sought to reconcile the poor to their lot: that poverty is good for the soul, that what is needful is enough, that eating little is nobler than eating more. Like early Socialism, the new creed was a creed of unexpected joy.

To restore this spirit of rapture to Socialism, this morning exhilaration, is something the theatre can help to achieve. I don't think it can happen if we are thinking of Socialism as a national movement, because national movements are seldom cheerful, any more than solitary men are cheerful: they grow rigid, resentful, xenophobic and defensive, like English Protestantism and Russian Communism. Socialism should be a gay international affirmation, a joint declaration that we are all equal members of a gigantic conspiracy to outwit the abysses of night and silence through which our planet coolly and predictably swings. It is not only a burning of weapons. It is a lighting of festal bonfires.

I am darting off into generalities, perhaps as a reaction against a theatre that is forever preoccupied with trivia. But it is only by iterating and reiterating the grand undeniable points that one can keep the drama aware of its full responsibility. Already, in the last few years, there has been a marked reduction in the number of unquestionably awful plays that have been produced in London. The biggest symbol of renaissance has been the experiment in planned repertory that began in the spring of 1956 at the Royal Court Theatre in Sloane Square, where we have seen works by Ionesco, Giraudoux, Arthur Miller and Carson McCullers, and where, more importantly, we were introduced to the first plays of Angus Wilson, Nigel Dennis and John Osborne. From this wellspring intelligent drama is seeping into the West End; slowly, of course, and lethargically, like ink across blotting-paper that has spent a generation in thick and petrified aridity.

* * *

A few months ago I tried to cram most of what I felt about this country into a long ironic letter written to a young man, the son of a friend of mine, who was coming to the end of his three years at Oxford, where he read English. It might be relevant here.

Dear John,

As one who has crossed the armed frontier that separates the university from real life, I feel a humane desire, now that you are on the eve of finals, to unload on you a little kindly advice. I do so because you are an arts student, and hence likely to be led into errors that might delay, perhaps indefinitely, your entry into the world of reality and success.

To begin with, it is important that you should realize your status. You are among the sixty per cent of undergraduates who are receiving financial aid from the state, and your position as such was defined, fearlessly and without equivocation, by Somerset Maugham in his Christmas 1955 message to the *Sunday Times*. 'They are scum,' he said: and since Mr Maugham rarely says anything controversial or uncertain of wide acceptance, I think you should heed his opinion. It is shared, I assure you, by many who lack his gift for plain speaking. I myself think that 'scum' is putting it a bit harshly, but you know how squeamish a thinker I am.

Before going on, I must admit to a deficiency. I know next to nothing about your generation at the university. Eight years have passed since I left Oxford, and we were pirates then, at least my friends were: an immodest band of unregenerate phonies all of whom, apart from myself, were ex-servicemen. We were mortal invalids and congenital nail-biters, and our figurehead was a stately necrophile who wrote in suave Trollopian periods about calamity and despair. One of his stories, I wince to remember, concerned a timorous hermit who awoke one day to find himself nailed inside a coffin that was being wheeled into a crematorium. Having passed through the flames, he emerged into a grey world of unimaginable horror, peopled with shambling zombies, which he took to be hell until a passing zombie told him it was Golders Green. From time to time we would beg our friend to cheer his fiction up, and one day he gave in: from now on, he said, the corpses would *dance*. That was the kind of person we were. All I can say for us is that, in an anarchic way and if you'll pardon the expression, we were democrats, though I doubt if many of us even then would have come out and shouted about it. The odd thing is that the 1945-48 generation did not mature at all badly. It is prominent in the Commons; it wrote a musical play that has been a hit on both sides of the Atlantic; it has influenced both kinds of television; it has made a telling mark in films, and it is said to have revivified the English novel. It even ran the first four-minute mile. And I cannot ignore its sluggards, many of whom have dropped some shapely pebbles into the puddles of Fleet Street.

Your case, of course, is different. Conditions applied in 1945 that cannot be repeated now. V-J day had just happened, and the pre-war order had not yet reasserted itself. Physically, we were cramped by rationing, but spiritually we had a lot of elbow-room. Authority was too busy to give us its full attention, and Class had not yet recovered (as, by God, it since has) from the dreadful wounds dealt it by the war. We were all profiting from a unique and transient phenomenon that swept across England in 1945. You will not remember it, but at the time we called it the Swing to the Left. (The Left used to be the opposite of the Right.) Now, as you know, moderation is the thing, and the '45-'50 period is regarded as the five lost years of middle-class masochism.

Several quite influential people told me in 1945 that if we had not gone to war against the wrong country the election results would have been much more sensible. This feeling has gained ground since then, especially inside the Establishment, and you must take care to study it. One of your soundest guides will be Evelyn Waugh, whom you need not tip. Consult and memorize the passage in his novel *Officers and Gentlemen* in which the hero, an officer and gentleman named Guy Crouchback, looks back longingly on the day when the Russo-German pact was signed and 'the Enemy was plain in view.' Now, alas, Hitler has invaded Russia, and Guy realizes, beyond all doubt, that Britain has been 'led blundering into dishonour'. Let me elucidate that last phrase. The dishonour to which it refers is that of allying ourselves with Russia instead of Germany. Get that quite clear. Guy Crouchback's attitude is all part of the middle-aged Swing to the Right, and it is something you will have to reckon with. You may leap on to the pendulum; you may duck; or you may hold your ground, in which case you will probably be caught a blinding blow behind the ear. If you risk that fate, my advice will have been in vain.

It is all a matter of attitudes. Your attitude towards your native land, for example, should be governed by a gracious old concept, redolent of all that was best in medievalism. Recently refurbished by Mr Waugh, it is called the concept of precedence. 'There is a single line,' he has written, 'extending from Windsor to Worm-wood Scrubs of individuals all justly and precisely graded.' Do not overlook the assumption behind the word 'justly'. Italicize it in your mind. It will help you to understand not only the meaning of justice but also the idea of a hierarchy as something fixed by God and not to be tampered with by you. You, as a writer, are a man in rebellion against an unchangeable order; you must never think of yourself as an organic part of a developing social entity.

A propos, I would recall to your mind a remark made two years ago by Anthony Nutting, when Krushchev and Bulganin were in India. His exact words have by now perished in a pulp-dump, or wherever old newspapers go for mashing, but the image he used was unforgettable. B. and K., he said, having been turned down at the front door, had gone round to the back. India, that is to say, was the tradesmen's entrance. I am not sure where the Jews stand in the Great Chain of Being; so many of them are so obstinately classless; but Windsor, of course, will stand always where it stands today, a permanent bulwark to protect the people against the depredations of feudalism.

Before you accept Lord Beaverbrook's offer, I think you should consider what it means to have a job on the *Daily Express*. You will have to learn how to write like a popular, excitable, middle-aged woman, who is easily flustered and something of a tease. You will quickly master the gasping, exclamatory style; but I bid you remember that this is the sister-organ of the *Sunday Express*, which told Guy Burgess that it 'would greatly appreciate' a few words from his pen, and then printed them alongside an editorial dismissing them as 'the propaganda of a pervert'. On the whole, I think you would be well advised to turn critic as soon as possible. Less schizophrenia is involved, and it is anyway safer to be among the watchers than among the watched. If, as will often happen, you dislike a book, play or film without knowing quite why, your best course is to accuse it of 'vulgarity' or 'bad taste'. These are the two great meaningless indispensables of English criticism. I have known writers who died penniless but happy in the know-ledge that they had never incurred them. Tell a man that he thinks loosely or writes irresponsibly, and you touch him not at all. Tell him that he writes badly, and he will scarcely know what you mean. But tell him that he is vulgar, tell him that he is tasteless, and you do more than wound him: you brand him an outcast for life.

We must now consider what your attitude towards foreigners should be. France is easy. Nancy Mitford answers the question, with her jubilant prostration at the feet of the French aristocracy. Russia is easier still: who could entertain anything but a sorrow-ing contempt for a country that has not only abolished nostalgia but made it impossible for money to breed? Towards America a little more ambivalence is customary. The thing to cling to is that Americans actively enjoy being insulted, and the old insults are still the best—'vulgar' and 'tasteless'. Americans abroad must always be approached with these two words, plus a faintly contemptuous smile, playing about one's lips. 'Vulgar', for instance, is the word for the remark made by the American humorist H. Allen Smith on seeing the playing-fields of Eton. 'Just to think!' he said. 'Here is where the battle of Yorktown was lost!'

Wisely ordained currency regulations will of course prevent you from seeing much of the Americans at home; but it is a fair inference that they are the same, if not worse. You should make a point of cultivating a lofty, frozen sneer for those occasions when Hollywood crops up in conversation. How typical is the gaudy brashness (brash is a key-word) of so-called 'musicals' such as *On the Town*! And how pathetically morbid the passion for self-exposure that turns out films like *On the Waterfront* and *Rebel Without a Cause*! Be passionately grateful that our film industry has escaped contamination. British movies never wallow in the sewers of realism, nor do they abuse their power over simple people's minds: not from them will you hear a word of serious criticism of the police, the civil service, the government, the armed forces or the educational system. We at least draw the line somewhere; you might even say, as a joke, that we draw it everywhere. And if Hollywood is a booby-trap, Broadway is nothing but a glossy receptacle for the outpourings of people like Clifford Odets, Lillian Hellman, Eugene O'Neill, Arthur Miller and Tennessee Williams.

Should you write a novel, do not omit to put an American into it. And when you do so, let the silver-tongued imps of satire grace your pen. Give him a name like Scab Dunz or Bum Schlum. (I could never have invented these: they sprang from Mr Waugh's inimitable imagination.) The name of Graham Greene's 'Quiet American' is Pyle, which paves the way for a killing little joke when the American asks the narrator why he does not address him by his Christian name. 'I'd rather not,' says the narrator: 'Pyle has got—associations.' Pyle is more than vulgar and tasteless: he is crew-cut and teetotal, and he blunders into violence before you can say *naïf*. He is ignorant of everything except air-conditioning, deodorants, internationalism and the other evils with which his country has burdened us. I could explode with rage when I hear people saying that *The Quiet American* is not a religious novel. It is intensely religious. It is the considered work of a man for whom the Devil has acquired a face—the face of America—and I am lost in admiration for the punctilio and energy with which the author, doing what he must, smashes it to pulp.

Here I must issue a warning. On no account read what are known as 'the better American magazines'. They will only fuzz your prejudices. They are all named after places, which stamps them provincial from the outset—*The Hudson Review*, *The Kenyon Review*, *The New Yorker*, and so forth. All you will find in them is a bright, blind devotion to accuracy, directness and unwounding wit. Their writers do not seem to be aware that prose is different in kind from conversation: the ghastly *ease* of their style proclaims their inability to comprehend the arts of well-bred circumlocution. *The New Yorker* in particular declines to be taught that good prose should be pitched at least an octave above reality. Why, in a recent issue it printed a story by somebody called J. D. Salinger, which dealt—on shiny paper among advertisements for cars and refrigerators—with the problem of perfect Christian love. There's vulgarity for you! And not one sentence that the admirers of Charles Morgan would recognize as literature.

If you feel unable to sympathize with any of these *idées reçues*, there is one other course open to you. I hesitate to mention it, for it is the most perilous of all. You *might* go out and discover what the rest of your generation is really like, and act on what you discover. It will astound and alarm you. Go first of all to the jazz clubs: we might even, if you want to risk it, make a rendezvous at one of them. You will first be surprised by the absence of the orgiastic frenzy you have been schooled to expect. You will notice that the dancers, quickly though they move, make contact only at the finger-tips. Sex comes later. Each deadpan partner stares, twirling, into the blue haze of smoke. Yet the whole place is explicitly alive. You will hear that London is rapidly becoming the jazz centre of Europe; that this is the only art in which our prestige is growing. And if you talk to the cats, you will find in them these qualities: an instinctive Leftism, an undemonstrative sympathy with anarchy, a dislike of classy politicians, a vivid vernacular made up of Hollywood, space fiction and local dialect, a polite interest in drugs, a good deal of shared promiscuous pleasure, and almost no drunkenness. These young people cannot look at Macmillan's face without laughing, and they cannot work up much interest in our inalienable right to flog Cypriot school-boys; though I feel they might be rather nettled if Liechtenstein were a Czarist colony and Russia sent over a *gauleiter* to enforce its loyalty. They are bright, unaggressive and authentically toler-ant. Few of them would be capable of doing anything with a razor except shaving with it. You could never make a lynch-mob out of them, because the art they live for was invented by negroes.

What they (and you, and I) lack is a rallying-point, social and political. They are classless; or, rather, they are drawn from every class except the top one. They need an organ, a platform to articulate their impatience with convention, with 'good taste', with 'British prestige', with the use of 'emotional' as a dirty word. You might give them their rallying-point, if you do not mind uphill battles. But I am forgetting. Having just been at a university, you will have had your taste for freedom soured by reading Arthur Koestler, the most brilliant and persuasive of the defeatists. You will have been overwhelmed by his skill in analogy, by his trick of equating individual behaviour with group behaviour; you will have learned that you have a love-hate relationship with America, that the French are suffering from ' collective amnesia ' about the German occupation, that your war-time admiration of Sir Winston's cigar was fetish-worship, that your Leftist sympathies are ' derived from adolescent revolt against the parents '. You may have concluded that the desire to iron out social inequalities is in itself a neurosis; and that the urge towards freedom is nothing but a birth-trauma. The time to read Koestler is after you have been defeated, not before. To read him before is to guarantee failure. You will not inspire my generation, or yours, by crying, with him, that ' we can at best hope for a reprieve.' The hell with that. We will not settle for life imprison-ment: we want a free pardon.

And we want it not just for ourselves, or our economic bloc, or our allies, but for our world. Do I speak for you when I ask for a society where people care more for what you have learned than for where you learned it; where people who think and people who work can share common assumptions and discuss them in the same idiom; where art connects instead of separating people; where people feel, as in that new Salinger story, that every fat woman on earth is Jesus Christ; and where those who carry the torch of freedom are never asked to run with it into the ammuni-tion dump? Do you want these things?

Perhaps you don't. In which case I must sign myself.

Your implacable enemy,

K.T.

I never posted the letter, because I heard that the boy had just signed a long-term contract with an advertising agency. There seemed no point in depressing him.

Ways without

a precedent

BILL HOPKINS

Bill Hopkins

Born in Cardiff, 1928. Mother a theatrical beauty, Violet Broderick, and father a Welsh actor, Ted Hopkins. 1944: joined the British United Press as sub-editor at the Ministry of Information. At eighteen was shipped to Germany for the Occupation. Demobbed 1949. Joined the Crusade for World Government for eighteen months as press officer and threw himself with immense fervour into the 'hopeless task of getting people to base their political thinking on the future'. Two years' travel on the Continent, writing poetry and articles. Came back and launched an ambitious weekly, *The Saturday Critic*. Lost all his money before the first number. Joined the *New York Times* London bureau and stayed for three years, resigning in 1956 to finish his first novel, *The Divine and the Decay* (publication autumn 1957). A second novel, *Time of Totality*, in preparation.

THE literature of the past ten years has been conspicuous for its total lack of direction, purpose and power. It has opened no new roads of imagination, created no monumental characters, and contributed nothing whatever to the vitality of the written word. The fact that the decade in question has shown the highest ratio of adult literacy in British history makes this inertia an astounding feat. So astounding, indeed, that the great majority of readers have turned their attention to the cinema, television and radio instead. Their reading talent has been commandeered by the more robust newspapers.

The truants can hardly be blamed for seeking livelier entertainment, since most writers have reduced themselves to the rank of ordinary entertainers, and for the most part, have failed to be even this. Writers see the shadow of the mass mortuary too clearly to provide good, knock-about entertainment. The same shadow prevents them from producing more enduring work by making nonsense of posterity.

All writers must accept this shadow across their consciousness as an occupational hazard, and its surmounting divides them cleanly into the camps of optimism or pessimism, allowing no shades of neutrality between. The negative acceptance has the strongest following just now, and for this reason the bulk of serious novels today almost inevitably offer victims as their cast and senseless brutality as their business. These works do not educate us a scrap, nor do they offer any great insights into the tumult of our time. The writers dwell instead on the horror of *anything* changing—man, mood or scene—and reveal that the precise value of all and everything is that it is here at present. The understanding is that Man is too frail and imperfect for violent change. It is a poor argument for literature, progress and health.

Unless there is a radical change in this outlook literature will continue its drift into negativism.

Many people have their own ideas of what a creative writer's job should be. The popular conception is that he should provide stories that are an escape from life. The slightest whiff of reality is regarded as an intrusion of the diabolical and an act of treachery. The ideal path amounts to improbable love yarns closing upon chaste kisses. If there is invariably an impoverished odour about these fabrications, the accolades of best-seller returns do not hint at it.

This view is not taken by the more intelligent, who demand a measure of truth with their entertainment. This again is asking for too little. The measure of truth dealt out is generally confined to obscene language in kitchen squalor and the dreary divesting of the heroine's virginity. Now unalloyed sex is a tedious business when it is repeated too often. But this is not borne out by the positive glut of literary prurience that has come our way over the past few years. As it shows no sign of stopping we must conclude either that the percentage of perverts is much higher than is imagined, or that there is nothing more pornographic than a half-truth. But, whichever it is, the fact remains that when it is only a small measure of truth that is requested, the result merely mirrors appearance. It never delves to the cause behind appearance. It is better to offer no truth at all than make this kind of compromise.

There are only a few who demand all the truth a writer possesses. Over the past twenty years, this demand was sufficient to encourage the development of Hermann Hesse and Thomas Mann, but few others of major creative stature. If the demand were extended to a larger and more perceptive audience it would doubtless encourage the emergence of even greater writers. Certainly it would produce a literature capable of vigorously advancing our present half-hearted ideas of living to an unprecedented level.

There is no likelihood of such an ideal audience coming into existence for the philanthropic purpose of encouraging a vigorous literature. This would be asking for a healthiness that does not exist among most intelligent people today. The same malady that prevents a vital literature from developing and becoming a regenerative force to our society, disposes of the idea of a sick audience transcending its condition and calling for chest expanders. Contemporary literature, whether on the printed page or declaimed from the boards of the theatre, shows its bankruptcy by confining itself to merely reporting on social conditions. It makes no attempt at judging them. Literature that faithfully reflects a mindless society is a mindless literature. If it is to be anything larger, it must systematically contradict the great bulk of prevalent ideas, offer saner alternatives, and take on a more speculative character than it has today. I am optimistic enough to think that immediately the results prove positive and exciting, the more conformist brands of literature will lose most of their following.

But the failure of literature is only a small part of a much wider catastrophe. When I refer to a lack of health among the intelligent, I touch upon what threatens the whole of our civilization with imminent collapse. The truth is that Man, for all his scientific virtuosity, cannot defeat his own exhaustion. To do so means drawing upon unused strengths that once would have been described as religious. Unfortunately, Man has become a rational animal; he rejects any suggestion of religiosity as scrupulously as an honest beggar denounces respectability. I say unfortunately, because it is mental and physical exhaustion that is the principal malady of our civilization. The very people who should be the leaders of our society are the most affected, so the disillusionment, despair and social revolt of our age has been allowed to grow unchecked.

All the problems and struggles that confront the growth of our civilization depend entirely on whether we can get an exhausted man back upon his feet and keep him there. If the answer is a negative one, our past counts for nothing: it has proved insufficient to preserve our future.

The reasons for this exhaustion are all documented and detailed in the archives of the past fifty years. Rationalism, Communism, Socialism, Labourism, Fascism, Nazism, Anarchism; the honest penny-ha'penny thinking that human happiness was an adequate goal, the quest for social equality; two world wars and a couple of dozen local blood-lettings; poison gas, tanks, aircraft, flame-throwers, atomic, hydrogen and cobalt bombs, bacteriological warfare; depressions, inflations, strikes . . . the documents are quite explicit and well known.

Altogether they amount to the exhaustion of a man with asthma having run a marathon race and found there were no trophies or glory at the end of it. That is exactly our own position. With every decade since the turn of the century we have intensified our endeavours while our condition has deteriorated. Now it seems that despite all our efforts, knowledge and hopes, besides the lives jettisoned in their millions, we have achieved nothing. The dry taste of futility lingers in the mouth of all. The energy of any flying spark is in itself enough to arouse popular amazement. The supineness of the intelligent is the tragic paradox of the Atomic Age. Only the insulated specialists, bafflingly capable of drawing the blinds against all other realities, remain enthusiastic about tomorrow.

The evidence of exhaustion stares out from the columns of the daily newspapers. The references to 'Angry Young Men' for example, record a general astonishment at the vigour of simply being angry. Another instance is the hero-worship of the late James Dean, who posthumously remains as the embodiment of Youth's violent rebuttal of a society grown pointless. That the rejection is equally pointless does not appear to matter; the sincerity redeems it. There is the idolization of such simple men as Frank Sinatra and Elvis Presley, the respective champions of wistful sentimentality and the stark voluptuousness of knowing one thing that's good, anyway. Which, after all, is one advantage of being a farmer's boy.

Significantly, the more thoughtful go only a few steps further to admire such writers as Samuel Beckett, Tennessee Williams and Arthur Miller. All of these playwrights have distinguished themselves for creating small men and women whose unlikely poetry is in their bewilderment in an inexplicable and often tyrannical world. The heroism of the Twentieth Century Man, as currently postulated, is : (a) in winning a compassionate pair of lips that will lull him to peace after an endless gauntlet of victimizations (thus mysteriously negating the lot), (b) kicking a bullying foreman (an enemy of the people) in a conclusive place, or (c) just inhabiting a dustbin with all the pretences down and stoically waiting for the end.

This is the landscape a new writer looks upon this year. Everything has deteriorated from the point in the mid-1940's we optimistically imagined to be already rock-bottom. What is left is a mockery of attempt, accomplishment and greatness.

It would be too easy to be angry and join the lynching parties. But this is not a writer's job. Nor is it for a writer to subscribe to the general bankruptcy, despair and apathy around him, whatever popularity might be obtained from it. If there *is* a task for the writer, it is to stand up higher than anyone else and discover the escape route to progress. His function is to find a way towards greater spiritual and mental health for his civilization in particular and his species in general. This is my own intention, and unless other writers adopt the same attitude our civilization will remain leaderless, lost and exhausted, and the chaos will continue until its eclipse under radio-active clouds.

Literature has been an accelerating factor to this state of affairs over the last decade. Instead of acting as a brake it has been intent upon glorifying the lostness, the smallness and the absolute impotence of Man under adverse conditions. This is the reverse of what its rôle must be in the future. It must begin to emphasize in every way possible that Man need not be the victim of circumstances unless he is too old, shattered or sick to be anything else. It is the conquest of external conditions that determines the extent of Mankind's difference from all other forms of life; and, in turn, decides the superiority of its leaders. If this is denied, then we are indeed due for elimination. Perhaps overdue. But contemporary writing will not bring itself to this assertion until it has been wrenched clear of its embrace with a falling society. The dismaying fact is, most writers seem quite satisfied to act out their present hysterical offices to the length of disaster itself. Their conversion is enough to set any salvationist with work to last several lifetimes.

It is customary for young writers to condemn those who have authority and influence. For my own part, I am unable to do this because I find their exhaustion only too understandable. The leaders of our civilization have strained at hopelessly impossible tasks for too long, and instead of creating a new structure for living, they have succeeded only in producing a succession of failures. Today they have reached a standstill, and the prospect of marshalling together one more attempt has become an outrage against all reason and experience.

They are reasonable men and their conclusion is, in the light of what they have done, entirely rational. If reason or rationalism can accept exhaustion, by the same terms ruin and death are equally acceptable. But survival is our inflexible rule of health; and since survival has become a completely irrational instinct, the time has arrived when we should look to the irrational for the means to reject this reasonable but (humanly speaking) unacceptable end of our civilization.

Firm upon this premise, I predict that within the next two or three decades we will see the end of pure rationalism as the foundation of our thinking. If we are to break out of our present encirclement, we must envisage Man from now on as superrational; that is, possessing an inner compass of certainty beyond all logic and reason, and ultimately far more valid.

The times we are entering require a far more flexible and powerful way of thinking than rationalism ever provided. Three sovereign states have been loosing hydrogen tests in the world's atmosphere in preparation for deterrent wars. Each new explosion shadow-boxes with genetical mutations in the coming generations. Populations everywhere are multiplying daily to that frightening point in the future when the earth's food resources will not be sufficient to supply all with one decent meal a day. The fish harvests from the oceans are diminishing. The problems of soil erosion and the reclamation of land swallowed up by water remain unattended. These are only a few of the more obvious questions that call for solutions on a new level. A level of universal planning that can only be encompassed by a supranational body like world government. Meanwhile, Science advances every year a trifle further beyond the comprehension of most of the human race.

The path of a civilization in our disorders leads directly to its extermination. And, while we take it, Proustians talk about their

sensitivity in dark rooms and stylists continue to manufacture their glittering sentences. This is the marrying of an illness to a deformity; a grotesque *mésalliance* to make even a lunatic marvel. But it will go on, as I say, until writers turn away and look objectively to another part of the horizon.

I have stated that Man is more than rational, and that if he is not, he is finished. Now I take the argument forward another step and assert that his current exhaustion is the vacuum created by an absence of belief. At the beginning of this credo I declared that only a religious strength could conquer exhaustion, and by religious strength I meant, specifically, belief: exhaustion exists only to a degree commensurate to its wane. A complete dearth of belief mathematically equates to utter exhaustion. It is no coincidence that it has struck the most responsible members of our society; they are the ones who have had the responsibility of scraping the barrel of reason and materialism. The same exhaustion will strike at the leaders of the East just as surely within a span of time roughly corresponding, no doubt, to our own venture into pure rationalism.

Through history, the men and women who have towered over their contemporaries through their achievements and struggles have had extraordinary levels of belief. They have ranged from visionaries, saints and mystics to fanatics and plain, self-professed, men-of-destiny. Whether their beliefs were in an external thing— let us say the Church—or simply in themselves, was a matter of little importance. The result in every case was sufficiently positive to make them memorable. Each of them was primarily separated from those around him by a greater capacity for belief. It took all of them high above the eternally small, grumbling, self-pitying parts that constitute personality. Belief is, and I speak historically, the instrument for projecting oneself beyond one's innate limitations. Reason, on the other hand, will have us acknowledge them, even when the recognition is disastrous, as now.

The admission of a permanent state of incompleteness has been made by a great many people and much of the damage I have referred to is the direct result of it. But their places have to be filled. It has become imperative that, just as a new way of thinking and a new literature are needed, a new leadership must also be evolved with the aim of combating this exhaustion by the restoration of belief.

When I speak of belief in the present context, I do not mean any belief in particular, of course, but rather belief divorced from all form whatsoever. The form is an arbitrary matter, and its choice in the sense of literature is essentially a matter for the writer's temperament. Whatever the choice, the reservoir of power within belief offers any writer the certainty of major work.

It is obvious that this concern with belief leads inevitably to the heroic. The two are joined as essentially as flight to birds. The hero is the primary condition of all moral education, and his reality is synonymous with any great idea. He is literally the personification of the dramatic concept. But the heroic poses the possibility of people who can think and act with a magnitude close to the superhuman. The introduction of such characters and events will require a great deal of care and skill, for the ridiculous is only one step away.

The greatest difficulty overhanging this work, however, will be in the motive force itself. There has been a nonsensical confusion between belief and religion that has lasted for centuries. Instead of belief finding its separate identity, it has always been inextricably tied to religion. Churches of every denomination deliberately fostered this misconception from their beginnings, for the belief latent in men responded to hot appeal and willingly testified to the truth of any proffered set of doctrines. The nature of belief appears to be conducive to appeals. Its generosity is evident in this respect when we examine many of the childish and absurd inventions the various religions have offered worshippers at one time or another.

It is quite true that the Church has been the only vehicle for belief on any sizeable scale up to the present, and deserves credit for it, although self-interest provided its own reward. But it is absurd to regard belief on the basis of tradition as the monopoly of any organization. The Church was the first to understand the potentialities of its power and was also the first to direct it to an end; but sole proprietary rights were assumed too rigidly for the Church to pass us now as a public benefactor. Those who tried to break the monopoly were decried as heretics. Where it could, the Church had them burnt. This confiscation of belief and its isolation under the steeple brought about the Reformation and eventually the George Foxes and other champions of the right to independent belief.

Over the past fifty years there has been a general rejection of all churches with the sole exception of the strongest, Catholicism. The rejection parcelled belief with the Church and disposed of both. It was the result of a considerable amount of ignorance and a distinct lack of subtlety. Today, the same excuses do not hold, and if the mistake is repeated, it can never be done with the same blind vehemence of the first rejection.

If this social exhaustion of ours is due to the rejection of belief, how can writers reclaim it? There are three choices open, at least. The first is the establishment of a new religion. The second, to revitalize and reconstruct Christianity. The third, to trace belief to its source and turn it to a new account.

The argument against the first is that a new religion, whatever advantages it would have (supposing for a moment that it should find an ample crop of visionaries, priests, theologians and militant doctrines), would suffer from its lack of tradition more than it would profit by its modernity. Although many people talk somewhat loosely about the need for a new religion, the very impossibility of it as an overnight phenomenon rules it out for today.

However, should this particular miracle come to pass, its contribution to our civilization would be a substantial one while it was sustained by its visionaries. But as soon as the visionaries died, its hierarchy would become rigid as precedents in the history of every church show us without exception. There would be no more room for succeeding visionaries with their tradition-breaking habits in this church than in any other.

A priest is a poor substitute for a visionary. So poor, in fact, that the plenitude of them against the paucity of visionaries has largely dissuaded many who with the right inspiration would be religious. A visionary has the prerogative of freely contradicting himself while still retaining his influence. Less flexible, because he happens to lack a visionary's imagination and vitality, the priest conscientiously commits to paper everything enunciated by the other in case he should forget the passport of his office. Subsequent

E

generations of priests accept the dogmas laid out for them without demur or question on the same grounds. This is orthodoxy; its strength is in its ossification. The more rigid the observance, the more virtuous the believer. . . .

There can be no prospect more terrible for any prophet coming after, and this is when a church really dies. When it is attacked from without, what is sent crashing is cardboard : the Church died after the passing of its first visionaries and the hardening of its arteries to fresh truths.

As this argues against the possibility of a new religion arising, it argues equally against the impossibility of a revitalized Christianity. Any great idea, if it is perpetuated without continual reappraisals, is eventually rendered into ritualistic twaddle and shibboleths that justify the cheapest sneers (although not the spirit) of its detractors. And finally, the sad truth is that the only men courageous enough to approach great ideas and test their truth are men of equal stature to their formulators. No church that I am aware of has produced an apostolic succession of this order, so we must put aside both possibilities as impractical for anyone who hopes to work within his own times.

The last alternative is the one that, under the circumstances, is the most realistic. If we can trace belief to its origins and examine it in terms of plain, unadorned power, we have a potential weapon that will play an immeasurable part in our salvaging. I am convinced that it is an internal power comparable, when fully released, to the external explosions of atomic energy. With a complete understanding of its nature, its functions and its strength at zenith, I believe that we can not only cure Man's many illnesses, but determine by its use a level of health never before attained. If we can learn the answers to these questions, Man may be transformed within a few years from the hardening corpse he has become into a completely alive being. The change can only be for the better.

One of the most tiring assumptions that has gained universality is that Man is completely plotted, explored and known. Dancing to the café orchestra of Darwin and Freud, there has been a tendency over the last fifty years to regard humanity as a fully arrived and established quantity that has little variation and no mystery to the scientist. Nothing could be more untrue. Man is so embryonic that attempting to define him today is preparing a fallacy for tomorrow. He is inchoate, only just beginning. Given unlimited belief and vitality, he is capable of all the impossibilities one cares to catalogue, including the most preposterous. Equally, without belief and vitality, he is simply decaying meat like any other fatally wounded animal. The difference will be largely decided by writers.

This is not a disproportionate claim. Writers have always influenced and led the thinking of their own times, immediately after the heads of State and Church. Sometimes, as with the Voltaires, a long way in front of either of them. The present heads of State are clearly unable to see a way through the difficulties of today, and there is no reason for us to suppose they can do any better with tomorrow. The non-existence of any influential Church leaders in Britain prohibits any criticism of their recalcitrance. The only remaining candidates qualified as leaders are writers.

The Greeks, unlike ourselves, expected their literary men to be thinkers and teachers as a matter of course. This expectation was justified by figures of the stature of Aeschylus, Sophocles and Euripides. Dramatists like these preached, taught, entertained and prophesied with such vitality and authority that their judgements were taken away by their audiences and applied to all levels of civic life. That both playwrights and audiences prospered upon this didactic relationship is best shown by the intellectual versatility of the Hellenic world, which has yet to be repeated.

When Bernard Shaw demanded that the theatre should be a church, he also meant that the ideal church should be a serious theatre. So it was in the Greek world. Nobody could afford to miss a sermon of this sort, because there was nothing more intellectually and spiritually exciting to be found from Kephallenia to far Samoso. Each new drama-sermon made the Kingdom of Man a titanic affair that could not be taken casually, and if this is not a religious understanding, there is no such thing!

In addition to this laudable state of sanity, they had none of the blank one-sidedness about them that stamps the orthodox priest, because their real religion was Man, and no other. Because Man is only human when he is in movement, they were able to throw him into catastrophic dilemmas that modern religion would regard as blasphemous. But they threw him only to retrieve him, and by this method they were able to add new understandings of his darker territories and enlarge his consciousness. With the aid of such dramatists the citizens of the Greek city-states developed into creditable human beings. But the high level of the theatre was to fall, and the whole of the Greek world was not long in following it.

When the Roman Empire rose to take its place, Terence and Seneca, the bright lights of Latin, reflected a frightening deterioration in what was expected of a writer. Julius Caesar found it an easy matter to be both a swashbuckler and a scribe in a world that, culturally, could not even conquer sculpture. But Rome's poverty was magnificence compared to the bankruptcy prevailing in Britain and everywhere else in the civilized world today.

However, when I call in history to augment my contentions I am beating upon a broken drum. The rôle I predict for writers is one entirely without precedent, and it is the better because of it. Aeschylus and his colleagues refined the Greeks, and that was quite enough for their day. But today writers must become the pathfinders to a new kind of civilization. That new civilization remains an impossibility until we extricate our own civilization from the destruction that threatens it.

The problem is that of the individual. What kind of man or woman survives cataclysmic events better than any others? What kind of people are the first to fall? What are the first disciplines necessary for a new, positive way of thinking? These questions, together with ten thousand others, fall into the kind of prophetic writing that will be needed to solve the problems that lie immediately ahead. The duty then of all writers who are concerned with tomorrow is to concentrate on defining human characters at differing stages of ideal health. From this gallery it will be possible for us to aim at men and women dynamically capable of laying the foundations of our new world. We may not be able to describe precisely the men and women we want, but at least we can provide a reasonable indication. We can narrow the perimeter of choice.

I realize that there is as great a difference between facts and speculations in the minds of writers as in the minds of ordinary people. The great difference is that writers are particularly suited to the correlation of apparently hostile facts, often blatant contradictions, and their craft teaches them to deepen and extend thoughts to final understandings that seem almost mystical to the average person. This talent to reach down into the depths of men and find appalling corruption, and far from being ruined by the revelation proceed to conceive supreme peaks of human perfection, is common to both writer and visionary. There is no reason why they should be different in other ways, if the dedication is strong enough.

Until now most writers have concerned themselves with recording the anomalies and cruelties perpetrated by a skinflint world upon a good small man. Modern literature, for lack of a great aim, has become a Valhalla for those who shriek, beat their brows and weep more energetically than anyone else. As a device, hysteria is very useful for a writer, but as an end it becomes patently ludicrous. Any writer who resorts to such tricks without offering a ticket of destination is wasting his own time and the time of his readers, flouting the *Zeitgeist* in the most imbecilic fashion, and finally (I hope) cutting his own throat.

The truth of today is too plain for clear-thinking people to ignore, however uncomfortable it may be to the inherently lazy. We must grow larger . . . see further and deeper . . . think with more skill, concentration and originality—or become extinct. If we are not capable of meeting these seemingly unattainable requirements, writers such as myself will persist obstinately in trying to have things as we want them even if the words are finally addressed to the abyss rather than human faces. If the crusade is a hopeless one, it will be so only because there is nothing more impregnable than human weakness. This is an important conclusion, and its recognition offers three salient truths.

First, that a writer's duty is to urge forward his society towards fuller responsibility, however incapable it may appear.

Second, a writer must take upon himself the duties of the visionary, the evangelist, the social leader and the teacher in the absence of other candidates.

Third, that he understands the impossible up-hill nature of a crusade and counters it by infusing in everything he creates a spirit of desperation.

This spirit of desperation is the closest approximation we can get to the religious fervour that brought about a large number of miraculous feats of previous, less reasonable, epochs. In desperation, as with religious exaltation, miracles, revelations and extraordinary personalities can be brought to everyday acceptance. The great advantage of it is that one can develop it to the point of being able to evoke it whenever there is cause for it.

I used the atmosphere of desperation in my first novel, *The Divine and the Decay*, very much in the way that a wind comes through an open door, throws a room into a sudden disarray, then leaves as abruptly. The wind in this case is a fanatic, and the room with an open door a small island community. As always in such cases, one is left perplexed and filled with a sense of indefinable outrage that has little to do with the disarray that must be restored to order. There is something maniacal about a really desperate man that welds him into a total unity and he becomes an embodiment of a single idea. Almost, dramatically speaking, flesh wrapped around an idea. Working for so long with desperation as my tool, I also learned about the merits of the lull, when the air vibrated with the foreboding of the next entrance. I relearned also a Greek lesson: how to turn presence into absence and absence into presence. But these details are worth mentioning only in relation to the use of desperation in contradistinction to the monotonous normality that most writers regard as the acme of reality.

Desperation is the only attitude that can galvanize us from this lethargic non-living of ours. But without a calculated direction desperation is useless. Misadventures in its application can leave us dangerously drained of further effort. This is where the dramatization of aims is expressly the writer's function. Consider the case of Sisyphus, whom the Gods had forever rolling that gigantic boulder of his up a hill and forever having it roll down again when he neared the top. The punishment was inflicted upon only too human strength. But with enough desperation the penalized king would not have attempted to roll it up after the first couple of attempts. He would have picked it up and *flung* it over the impossible crest, straight into the faces of his Olympian tormentors. I can think of many contemporary equivalents of the Sisyphean plight that are incessant defeats only because each of the sufferers refuses to rear up and wreck his opposition with the fury of desperation. To me, desperation is our immediate instrument, in the absence of belief, for collapsing this damnable, subhuman recognition of one's surface limitations. Refuse to acknowledge them and the horizon spreads wide.

This cannot be done without examples, as I have said. The examples themselves can only be set by fanatics advancing beyond the arena of human experience and knowledge. In a religious sense, the fanatic or writer goes into the wilderness, the first act of any visionary's apprenticeship. Simultaneously, he becomes a social leader also, for humanity having to travel beyond the point where it now rests will only use paths already trodden.

New paths can only be created by writers with a desperate sense of responsibility. The only others capable of such a task are religious and philosophic minds, but unfortunately orthodoxy has ruined the first, and a desiccation debars the second. In resting the responsibility of human deliverance upon writers I am not calling for miraculous transitions antipathetic to their nature. Fundamentally, the writer has always been a prophet and a diviner in embryo. Centuries of 'telling a jolly tale' have simply caused him to let these other parts fall into disuse. I want their return, and I want them cultivated to full growth.

At the moment, the position of the writer in society is a difficult one. The good ones feel, quite rightly, that they should be antagonistic to authority; but the feeling is only a feeling and remains nothing more because few have got around to the point where they must begin wrestling with it. Because of this apprehension which is not turned into positive action, these writers find themselves nullified and abortive. They try to offset this predicament by an over-haughty pride in their isolation. More specifically they emphasize their artistic position to offset shortened powers, and offer a defensive façade of being icy intellectual pinnacles which, in actuality, spells death to their work if this attitude is carried to their desks.

To be exact, a writer is rather a ludicrous figure at work. He must be, to put himself in an arena with berserk bulls to gauge how much damage the horns can do. The gorings constitute literally the blood and tissue of his work; they are part of his empirical research into life. Perhaps research is too dignified a term for the tattered and bloody creature he becomes if he persists until he reaches the level of a good writer.

By such voluntary acts, he becomes an authority on the most fundamental subjects. Pain, for instance. It is not the politician, theologian or doctor who catalogues the depth, the range and the gamut of it, but the writer. He can state from personal knowledge that it has a hundred different pages, all written in different inks. Similarly, he is an expert in regions like agony, happiness, terror, exultation and whirling hope. These are his working neighbourhoods.

He also knows from personal experiment the fine shades of violence; its velocity, trajectory and impact; its sources, and its quivering conclusions. When an accident is about to happen, let us say an aeroplane is plunging in a death dive, or a child is about to go under the wheels of a motor car, most eyes will be averted until it is over. But this is a luxury a writer simply cannot afford, and he will watch even if the object of study is someone he loves intensely. He has conditioned himself to observe everything that happens within his orbit with a steady and remembering eye. As his craft is produced at first-hand, constantly in positions of physical and mental hardship, for him the step towards vision and leadership is not a large one.

On the face of it, it seems ironical that a writer who goes to such lengths to learn this abnormal craft should use it only for the purpose of entertaining. But most are given little choice to be anything else with the shadow of destruction hanging over them. The few writers who would like to create heroic work are discouraged in advance, for they cannot be sure of even polite credulity on the part of readers. All ambitious contemporary writers are haunted by the thin, peaky face of the rational reader who peruses his literature with the pursed lips of a confirmed sceptic. Anything larger than his own life is anathema to this gentleman. Authors know it well and go in dread of him. This is why only a foolhardy few dare create anything but the slightest, most prosaic structures. The heroic, the bizarre, the moral and religious fabrics, have been torn down in the interests of reality. If the realities were large there would be little ground for complaint, but what is considered to be real by the normal canons of judgement is, of course, as confined as candlelight. It is not surprising that creative thinking today operates upon candle-power.

The situation is so bad that many leading writers have fallen to mocking their own ability to serve 'fodder to pygmies'. They are proud of the ingeniousness they have developed over the course of time in feeding sly pieces of originality with every hundredth spoonful, done so skilfully it passes almost unnoticed. It is the bare remnants of creative pride. In another age a man could be a master; today he must be a midget, breathing a sigh of relief every time he gets away with his creative crime unpunished. This attitude of contemptuous hostility between writers and readers is another symptom of the need for a rupture between life and literature. The writer cannot create as largely as he wants; the reader is incapable of belief. Unless this stalemate is broken and another game started, the chess pieces will be swept to the floor. . . .

Let me take you into the theatre and make an illustration of tragedy. An infinite number of creators have visited this terrain for the purpose of laying their masterpieces. It is as studded with great monuments as a war cemetery. On one you will read *Prometheus Bound*, next to it, *Agamemnon*. Close by perhaps *Oedipus Rex*, and, among the newer additions, *Hamlet*, *Macbeth* and *Faust*. Death . . . broken dreams . . . disillusion. . . . There are a thousand threads in the pattern of it, and no doubt there are persons who walk the streets of London, Berlin and New York with threads still unwound and unwritten in their minds. But tragedy, with all the multiplicity of permutations before its inevitable curtain, has one basic demand. The downfall.

My difficulty is in imagining how an object can fall in any direction other than down. However, most thinking people today appear to find more difficulty in imagining any height superior to themselves. That brings us to the dilemma. If a tragic figure is to fall he obviously cannot fall a few inches and hope to capture our awe or our pity; his fall must be a considerable one. It never is,

E*

under the present conditions. As soon as the figure of prospective tragedy begins to climb over the heads of his audience, they insist he climb down again to a height where they can believe in him. The only exception to this is *Jack and the Beanstalk*. And Jack only gets away with it, I surmise, because his pantomime appears in the Christian season of drunkenness and makes a swift departure before sober judgements are restored.

If a hero cannot rise, he cannot fall; on this point of order such good rationalists as Galileo, Newton and Einstein will bear me out. Such a fall would be unnatural, ungravitational and illogical; in fact, there is no fall. And yet Tragedy must have it.

Very well, what is it that sets the proper height for a tragic descent? Put in this way, it is like discussing a ballerina's artistry in terms of ballistics! Let us assert, however, that tragedy has always demanded the greatest height conceivable as an essential condition of the downfall. A lot of levels contribute to make up this total height. The height is created by an outraged spiritual understanding, a shattered moral code and the complete social abasement of the protagonist. The downfall is darker than death; and often death is willingly chosen in preference to it, indeed as the very palliative of it when the intensity of anguish produced becomes fully manifest.

But these platforms of consciousness are ridiculously archaic to the modern world. The religious, moral and social heights have become melodramatic and unintelligent, beside the more modern concentration on the significance of a man's facial twitches under psychoanalysis. For that, we have banged our windows shut on Heaven and locked the cellar door on Hell. We have foreshortened our intelligence accordingly. The result is that *Oedipus Rex*, *Prometheus Bound*, *Hamlet*, *Macbeth* and *Faust* would not only be laughed out of our London theatres if they were written today but, in truth, would be impossible to write today unless my thesis for creating fresh belief finds more general acceptance. Until it has, our own contribution to tragedy's magnificent cemetery is a headstone inscribed: *No More Tragedies*. By it, we have created a tragedy infinitely more tragic than anything by Aeschylus, Shakespeare or Goethe.

The only indulgence to tragedy on the London stage is accorded to Shakespeare, whose vintage has removed him beyond the critical appraisals of the *cognoscenti*. The Shakespearian seasons that continue *ad nauseam* in the Waterloo Road serve as final evidence that the only good writer is a dead one. While the Old Vic flourishes as a salve to the national conscience, the absence of new tragedy is concealed from all but those who love and care for the theatre. The phenomenon of the Old Vic is the story of the orthodox Church hardening its arteries against fresh truths all over again. Just as the Church is content with past visionaries and anachronistic dogmas, the theatre brandishes dead playwrights as its testament of greatness. In either case the result is bad. The sad and obvious truth about the titans of the past is that Aeschylus did not know the meaning of world over-population; Goethe was in the dark about guided missiles; Shakespeare was a complete idiot on the question of nuclear fission. The only writers competent to deal with these present-day problems are writers who are alive!

I believe that this civilization of ours requires cement to stop its crash until a new civilization is developed. Its great need, ultimately, is for a new religion to give it strength. In the meantime we urgently need a philosophy to span the gaps in our society that grow wider every day. But a philosophy and a religion can be evolved only by a new leadership. The possibility of such leaders depends solely on whether we can produce men capable of thinking without rule or precedent. Apart from writers with phenomenal powers of dedication, I cannot see the likelihood of such men emerging in time to meet the oncoming crises.

For these reasons, I believe that literature must be the cradle of our future religion, philosophy and leadership. In this belief I see the writer filling the paramount rôle if our civilization is to survive.

Get out
and push!

LINDSAY ANDERSON

Lindsay Anderson

Born in 1923, Bangalore, South India. Scots parents. Classical scholar Wadham College, Oxford. Has written a good deal of film criticism for *Sight and Sound, The Times, Observer,* and *New Statesman and Nation.* Founder editor of the film review *Sequence* (1947–51). Has written one book, *Making a Film,* 1952. Worked on several experimental productions, including James Broughton's *The Pleasure Garden* (as producer), and Lorenza Mazzetti's *Together* (editor); both these films prized at Cannes, 1954 and 1956. Own films include *Wakefield Express* (1953); *Trunk Conveyor* (1954); *Thursday's Children* (in collaboration with Guy Brenton: American Academy Award for best documentary short, 1955); *Foot and Mouth* (for Ministry of Agriculture); *Henry* (for N.S.P.C.C.). Directed some of Robin Hood television films, 1956. Involved in *Free Cinema* movement at the National Film Theatre 1956–7: own contributions *O Dreamland,* and *Every Day Except Christmas,* documentary short about Covent Garden Market, which won Grand Prix at Venice, 1957. Directed Kathleen Sully's *The Waiting of Lester Abbs* for the English Stage Society at the Royal Court Theatre, 1957.

O for a single hour of that Dundee,
Who on that day the word of onset gave!

Let's face it; coming back to Britain is always something of an ordeal. It ought not to be, but it is. And you don't have to be a snob to feel it. It isn't just the food, the sauce bottles on the café tables, and the chips with everything. It isn't just saying goodbye to wine, goodbye to sunshine. After all, there are things that matter even more than these; and returning from the Continent, today in 1957, we feel these strongly too. A certain, civilized (as opposed to cultured) quality in everyday life: a certain humour: an atmosphere of tolerance, decency and relaxation. A solidity, even a warmth. We have come home. But the price we pay is high.

For coming back to Britain is also, in many respects, like going back to the nursery. The outside world, the dangerous world, is shut away: its sounds are muffled. Cretonne curtains are drawn, with a pretty pattern on them of the Queen and her fairy-tale Prince, riding to Westminster in a golden coach. Nanny lights the fire, and sits herself down with a nice cup of tea and yesterday's *Daily Express*; but she keeps half an eye on us too, as we bring out our trophies from abroad, the books and pictures we have managed to get past the customs. (Nanny has a pair of scissors handy, to cut out anything it wouldn't be right for children to see.) The clock ticks on. The servants are all downstairs, watching T.V. Mummy and Daddy have gone to the new Noel Coward at the Globe. Sometimes there is a bang from the street outside—a backfire, says Nanny. Sometimes there's a scream from the cellar —Nanny's lips tighten, but she doesn't say anything. . . . Is it to be wondered at that, from time to time, a window is found open, and the family is diminished by one? We hear of him later sometimes, living in a penthouse in New York, or a *dacha* near Moscow. If he does really well, he is invited home, years later, and given tea in the drawing room, and we are told to call him Professor.

It is a cosy enough fantasy, if you like that sort of thing. But unfortunately fantasy tends to become confused with reality, when enough people surrender to it: and this is what seems to have happened here. The only trouble is, we are not alone in the world. We are not even as far away from the rest of it as we used to be. Sometimes the old house trembles, when one of those backfires goes off particularly hard; but if you suggest a bit of rebuilding, you are looked at as though you've said something disgusting. Why is this? I ask myself. Do people doubt that we have the capacity to re-shape, re-invigorate, to adapt ourselves to the changed conditions of our time? Certainly far too many of us, and particularly those who speak with any kind of authority, seem to be anxiously obsessed about the ' Greatness ' of Britain— and to be able to conceive it only in terms of the past. One remembers those nostalgic headlines in the *Daily Sketch* : EDEN GETS TOUGH. SAYS ' HANDS OFF OUR CANAL '. IT'S *Great* BRITAIN AGAIN !

*   *   *

I work in the cinema, which gives me a further reason for despondency when I return to Britain. Admittedly this is a difficult enough medium to work in anywhere, but in few other parts of the world is so little significant use made of it. My most recent visit to the Continent was to the Tenth International Film Festival at Cannes. We saw films from some thirty-five countries, from East and West, Right and Left. And really, after a winter in London, it was astonishing to find the amount of responsible, meaningful work being done by film-makers in the world outside: humanism breaking through, in Russian pictures as well as American, in films which cost practically nothing from Ceylon as well as in the big-budget affairs from France, Italy and Japan. Prizes went to Poland, Sweden, France, America, Russia, Rumania, Japan, Yugoslavia. . . . Britain did not figure in the list. It is six years since a British feature won a prize at Cannes. And this is not the result of political or economic intrigue: it is a fair reflection of the way our films have fallen out of the running. The cinema reflects, much more immediately than most of the arts, the climate and spirit of a nation. Abroad particularly, where one gains that extra measure of objectivity, it is alarming to see what we produce, what we put up with.

What sort of cinema have we got in Britain? First of all it is necessary to point out that it is an *English* cinema (and Southern English at that), metropolitan in attitude, and entirely middle-class. This combination gives it, to be fair, a few quite amiable qualities: a tolerance, a kind of benignity, a lack of pomposity, an easy-going good nature. But a resolution never to be discovered taking things too seriously can soon become a vice rather than a virtue, particularly when the ship is in danger of going down. To counterbalance the rather tepid humanism of our cinema, it must also be said that it is snobbish, anti-intelligent, emotionally inhibited, wilfully blind to the conditions and problems of the present, dedicated to an out-of-date, exhausted national ideal.

These are all quite familiar middle-class—or more precisely upper middle-class—characteristics. Now I know that to many people, mention of 'class' always seems to be in bad taste. We are supposed to have risen above all that sort of thing. But we haven't. The grim truth is that we still live in one of the most class-conscious societies in the world, and I see nothing to be gained from the pretence that this is no longer so. The only way, in fact, we can usefully communicate with each other is by being honest about our backgrounds and our inherited prejudices. (This is not the same thing as saying we should hang on to them.) So I state here that I am fully qualified to talk about upper middle-class characteristics, because that is the class into which I was born. My father was an Army officer, and my mother the daughter of a wool-merchant. I was educated at a preparatory school on the South Coast, and at a West Country public school. (*Floruit, floret, floreat....*) Thus, though I dislike as much as anyone the smarty left-wing dismissal of all sentiments of patriotism or fair-play as Public School juvenilia, I need no prompting to admit that most of these characteristics we are discussing stem directly from our upper-class system of education.

The snobbery of our films is not aristocratic. In British films the aristocracy is generally represented by Mr A. E. Matthews, and is treated, though respectfully, as a fine old figure of fun. Similarly, the functions of working-class characters are chiefly comic, where

they are not villainous. They make excellent servants, good tradesmen, and first-class soldiers. On the march, in slit trenches, below
decks, they crack their funny Cockney jokes or think about the
mountains of Wales. They die well, often with a last, mumbled
message on their lips to the girl they left behind them in the Old
Kent Road, but it is up there on the Bridge that the game is really
played, as the officers raise binoculars repeatedly to their eyes,
converse in clipped monosyllables (the British cinema has never
recovered from Noel Coward as Captain 'D'), and win the battles.
A young actor with a regional or a Cockney accent had better
lose it quick: for with it he will never be able to wear gold braid
round his sleeve—and then where are his chances of stardom?

Most people are innocently unaware of the way this kind of
snobbery restricts our cinema, as it does our theatre too. I suppose
this is because it is so very English in its tone, and therefore
whimsical, indulgent and unselfconscious, never violent and seldom aggressive; never imagining that it could arouse resentment;
sublimely convinced that it reflects the natural order of things.
There are elements of truth, even, in its stereotypes; but their
untruth is far greater. It is, up to a point, reasonable to show
British people as, on the whole, more equable than Italians: but
it is merely libellous to insist that our emotions are so bottled up
that they have ceased to exist at all. You know the sort of thing.
Mrs Huggett, the policeman's wife, is told of her husband's death
in the course of duty. (He has been knifed while attempting to
arrest a Teddy Boy for dancing rock-and-roll on the pavement at
the Elephant and Castle.) There is a pause, pregnant with nothing.
Then Mrs Huggett speaks, quiet and controlled: 'I'll just put
these flowers in water.' Polite critical applause for another piece
of truly British understatement. English film makers, to quote Roy
Campbell, use the snaffle and the bit all right—but where's the
bloody horse? (The horse, naturally, is out in the stable, round at
the back of the house. And that's where we've been told not to
go.)

The number of British films that have ever made a genuine try
at a story in a popular milieu, with working-class characters all
through, can be counted on the fingers of one hand; and they have
become rarer, not more frequent, since the war. Carol Reed's film

of *The Stars Look Down*, made in 1939, looks somewhat factitious today; but compared with his *A Kid for Two Farthings* two years ago, it is a triumph of neo-realism. The real objection, though, is not so much that 'popular' subjects are falsified, as that they are not made at all. Quite recently a friend of mine took a story to a distributor to find out if he would agree to handle the film if it were made. (It is these middlemen, incidentally, who decide what reaches the screen in Britain, not the producers or the public.) The reaction was illuminating. It was a story of working-class people, and it opened in a garage yard, with the men sitting in the sun, eating their lunch-hour sandwiches. One of them, a boy of sixteen, has a cold and needs to wipe his nose. 'For pity's sake, get your snot rag out,' grumbles one of his mates. The distributor's decision was unequivocal, and its grounds clearly expressed. 'It starts on that social level, and it never rises above it. Audiences just don't want to see that sort of thing.' And this is why—even if the talent to make them were around—equivalents of *Marty* and *The Grapes of Wrath*, *Two Pennyworth of Hope* and *The Childhood of Maxim Gorky* cannot be produced in this England.

This virtual rejection of three-quarters of the population of this country represents more than a ridiculous impoverishment of the cinema. It is characteristic of a flight from contemporary reality by a whole, influential section of the community. And, which is worse, by reason of their control of the cinema, they succeed in imposing their distorted view of the present on their massive and impressionable audience. According to the testimony of our film-makers (the oath is administered by the Censor), Britain is a country without problems, in which no essential changes have occurred for the last fifty years, and which still remains the centre of an Empire on which the sun will never have the bad manners to set. Nothing is more significant of this determination to go on living in the past than the succession of war films which British studios have been turning out for the last four or five years, and which shows no sign of coming to an end. Now of course there are many different ways of making films about war. You can make a film like *All Quiet on the Western Front*, which is an out-cry against the whole abomination. Our war films are not like that. Or, like the Poles in the last few years, you can keep return-

ing to the war because you are obsessed by it; because it crystal-
lized a conflict, an essential aspiration; because it evokes ghosts
that have to be exorcized. But when the Poles showed *Kanal* at
Cannes, they prefaced it with an announcement. ' This film,' they
said, ' is not made as an exciting entertainment. It is made as a
reminder of what occurred, and as a warning, that such things
should not be allowed to happen again.' We do not make war
films like this either. These stories continue to be made in Britain
firstly because they are profitable. Secondly, because the world of
the services is one which perpetuates the traditional social set-up
of the country, its distinctions of class and privilege. And thirdly,
because by escaping into war, we can evade the complex uncer-
tainties of the present, and the challenge of the future. Back there,
chasing the *Graf Spee* again in the Battle of the River Plate, tapping
our feet to the March of the Dam Busters, we can make believe
that our issues are simple ones—it's *Great* Britain again!

In 1945, it is often said, we had our revolution. It is true we
had something; though for a revolution it was a little incomplete.
According to the British cinema, however, nothing happened at
all. The nationalization of the coal fields; the Health Service;
nationalized railways; compulsory secondary education—events
like these, which cry out to be interpreted in human terms, have
produced no films. Nor have many of the problems which have
bothered us in the last ten years: strikes; Teddy Boys; nuclear
tests; the loyalties of scientists; the insolence of bureaucracy. . . .
The presence of American troops among us has gone practically
unremarked; so have the miners from Italy and the refugees from
Hungary. It is only with reference to facts such as these, that
criticism of British films can now have any relevance; for, on the
present level, aesthetic discussion can hardly be more than a game.
What we need to consider is the image of ourselves that our
cinema is bent on creating, and whether we, as a nation, should
continue to accept that image. Further, we must question the
significance, and the justice, of the use those in political and
financial control of us are content to make of this powerful,
essentially democratic medium.

The cinema is an industry. This is a statement which no one is
likely to contest. It is also an art—and most people will allow that

too. But it is something else as well: it is a means of communication, of making connexions. Now this makes it peculiarly relevant
to a problem of the most urgent importance to us—and it is
admitted to be so by both of our effective political parties. I mean
the problem of community—the need for a sense of belonging
together—of being prepared to make sacrifices for the common
good. Naturally, it is only in difficult times that we hear these
principles invoked by politicians. Then: 'All hands to the
pumps!' they call. But it is no use expecting to find the deck
hands running unless they have been made to feel, earlier in the
voyage, that the ship is theirs, and worth their trouble to save.
That they are a part of it. One of the most powerful ways of
helping people to feel this is by making films. There was a time
when this was understood in this country, at least by a few. In
the thirties the British documentary movement, led by John
Grierson, built up a tradition of good, social-democratic film-
making. And when the war came, and the G.P.O. Unit could be
transformed directly into Crown Film Unit, the nation was very
happy to reap the benefit. During a war it is useful to be able to
appeal to national democratic sentiments. ('Your courage, your
hard work, your cheerfulness will bring Us victory!' as that
unfortunate poster put it.) But after a war, when the slogan is
'Back to Business as Usual!' democratic sentiments are apt to
seem unnecessary, and such appeals are discontinued. It is true
that Crown continued to function for a time, making films about
health, about education, about the national economy; but this was
under the Labour Government. With the return of the Tories, in
1951, the unit was disbanded. It had become a luxury. And today
it is practically impossible to make films of this kind in Britain.
There is no money for them (except in rare and special cases) from
the Treasury. They are not wanted by the men who book for the
circuit cinemas. Their speculative production is out of the question. Who are the losers by this situation—the business men? Or
the community?

*   *   *

'It is vitally important that words like Duty and Service should
come back into fashion. . . .' So Lord Hailsham told the nation

in a recent political broadcast. But questions prompt themselves: Duty to whom, and why? Service to what ideal? One is again reminded of that wartime poster. And when Mr Macmillan, making his first broadcast as Prime Minister, talks about 'dreary equality', we recognize the concept of society that inspires him. We are back with the hierarchy, the self-idealized *élite* of class and wealth, the docile middle-classes, and the industrious, devoted army of workers. 'All things Bright and Beautiful. . . .' 'The Rich Man in his Castle, the Poor Man at his Gate. . . .' 'Wider still and wider Shall thy Bounds be set. . . .' These are the songs Mr Macmillan will lead us in, with additional verses by Sir Arthur Bryant and A. L. Rowse, and *The Times* to lead the admonitory choruses:

'All this is a part of a deplorable flight from responsibility which has sapped so much of the effectiveness both of our national life and our international position. Other nations do not realize that it is easier for us to blame ourselves, and that while we are generally masters of understatement, this does not apply where our conscience is concerned.'

Fine words. . . . They come from that celebrated leader—'Escapers' Club', it was headed—in which *The Times* rebuked those who suggested that Nasser's seizure of *Suez* was being injudiciously handled by the Government ('a deplorable flight from responsibility'). It was a call to greatness indeed. It ended:

'Doubtless it is good to have a flourishing tourist trade, to win Test matches, and be regaled by photographs of MISS DIANA DORS being pushed into a swimming pool. But nations do not live by circuses alone. The people, in their silent way, know this better than the critics. They still want Britain great.'

A classic expression, this, of the Tory mentality, proudly blinkered to the last. Images of tourism, sport and a corrupt entertainment industry are lumped together as symbolizing popular culture, and dismissed. And what is the alternative by which the People (in their respectfully silent way) are to be inspired? The attack on Egypt provided the answer.

But it won't do. By now, surely, even *The Times* must have gathered that this kind of antique notion of greatness is simply

out of date. Fundamentally, our problems today are all problems
of adjustment: we have somehow to evolve new social relationships within the nation, and a new relationship altogether with
the world outside. Britain—an industrial, imperialist country
that has lost its economic superiority and its empire, has yet to
find, or to accept, its new identity. The irresolution expresses itself
widely, and in many different ways: in discontent or opportunism
among young people, in nostalgic complaints and futile bombast
from the established Right, and in a weary shrugging of the
shoulders from those who were Pink, or even Red, twenty years
ago. But the real question remains unanswered. If 'Land of Hope
and Glory' is to be decently shelved, what song are we to sing?

In literal as well as metaphorical terms, the answer of the Left
is so far inadequate. I have rarely heard a more depressing sound
than the singing of those few, indomitable, old-fashioned Leftists
who raised their voices in chorus at the end of the Suez demonstration in Trafalgar Square:

> *Let cowards flinch and traitors sneer—*
> *We'll keep the Red Flag flying here.* . . .

It was more of a moan than a song; and no wonder. For how can
a tired old vision like this expect to win new allegiances today?

I am not going to say that the British Labour movement is as
out of touch with the present as the Tories. Their stake is in the
future, and they are under no such temptation to romanticize the
past. But their failure of imagination has been hardly less disastrous. The old, moral inspiration of radicalism has dribbled
away, and its loss has certainly not been made good by Fabian
intellectualism. The trade Unions are as capable of philistine,
narrowly sectional actions as the Tories—perhaps even more so.
The internationalism of the Left was not strong enough to extend
open and unqualified help even to the Hungarian miners; and in
place of a forthright appeal to the common sense and conscience
of the nation, the Labour Party descended at the last General
Election to a campaign frankly bourgeois and paternalistic in its
inspiration: the chintz armchair—the Premier with his Pipe—
'You can trust Mr Attlee!' They deserved to lose.

We have a thousand problems to resolve in this country, but

the essential one is this: What kind of Britain do we want? What ideal are we going to set ourselves in our re-ordering of society? What truths do *we* hold to be self-evident? These are not abstract questions, nor even political questions in any professional sense: their answers will affect the lives and work of all of us who do not regard ourselves as predestined outsiders. At least the Tory position is frank, with its rejection of equality as a 'dreary' ideal, and its determination to return to the old way of a privileged society and a capitalist economy. It is Socialism which has yet to present its solution dynamically, to shake off its complexes of inferiority and opposition, to speak with confidence, and from the heart. We are still between Arnold's two worlds, one dead, the other powerless to be born; and the frustrated exasperation that inevitably results, particularly among the young and ardent, has been one of the most significant phenomena of recent years:

'There aren't any good, brave causes left. If the big bang does come, and we all get killed off, it won't be in aid of the old-fashioned, grand design. It'll just be for the Brave New-nothing-very-much-thank-you. . . .'

It was at this point in *Look Back in Anger* that a friend of mine wanted to jump to his feet and call out: 'What about Suez?' I knew what he meant, but it would have been a silly thing to do. John Osborne could, of course, have made Jimmy Porter a resolute and positive Leftist, but in that case he would have written a different play—and, things being what they are, probably a less interesting one. It would also be a great deal too facile to dismiss Jimmy Porter's angry point of view as merely the rationalization of his neurosis: this is what most of the elder critics attempted to do, in their reluctance, or their inability, to interpret the portents. ('A young man at the centre of the stage, self-pitying, attitudinizing, talks at length, cheaply violently, foolishly. . . .'—Mr J. C. Trewin.) But the public came; and largely a young public. What did they see? Not merely, it is obvious, the hysterical boor which is all the central character could seem to the middle-aged, unperceptive eye; but a tremendously forceful expression of their own disgust with contemporary hypocrisies, and at the same time a reflection of their own sense of confusion and lack of focus. This was the heartening thing: that here at last was a young writer, using the language of today, giving passionate expression to his uncertainty and his frustrated idealism—and being received by his contemporaries at least, with understanding and enthusiasm.

It is not really Osborne's anger that is significant, so much as the complement of it: his baffled aspiration, his insistent plea for a human commitment. These are qualities that have been out of fashion for a long time. Indeed it is ironic to find Osborne's name linked journalistically (as an 'angry young man') with two other writers who are fashionable precisely because they express the directly opposite attitude to his own. Both Kingsley Amis and John Wain have a certain satirical view of society which gives them a remote affinity to Jimmy Porter; but basically they are both of them anti-idealist, anti-emotional, and tepid or evasive about their social commitments. It is because they are so depressingly representative in all this of what we may call the *Liberal* establishment, that I think it is worth while considering one or two of their characteristic statements in some detail.

Amis has perhaps been the most honest. In an extremely illuminating pamphlet issued by the Fabian Society (*Socialism and the Intellectuals*), he has done his best to define his position. He is discussing what he calls 'a quality as characteristic of the Fifties intellectual as of his predecessor in the Thirties':

'Romanticism in a political context I would define as an irrational capacity to become inflamed by interests and causes that are not one's own, that are outside oneself. If this sounds hostile or bad-tempered, I had better say at once that I see myself as a sufferer from political romanticism just as much as the next man. Anyway, by his station in society the member of the intelligentsia really has no political interests to defend, except the very general one (the one he most often forgets) of not finding himself bossed around by a totalitarian government. . . . Furthermore he belongs to no social group which might lend him stability; his only group is the intelligentsia itself, where stability is associated mainly with alcoholic coma. In these circumstances our intellectual shops around for a group and for a cause to get excited for.'

In a passage like this, most of Amis's attitudes are clearly illustrated: they are unattractive, but they are fashionable. They are also expressed with astonishing poverty of thought and looseness of language. Consider this 'definition' of political romanticism: 'irrational' in the first sentence is simply question-begging, and phrases like 'not one's own' and 'outside oneself' are meaningless as they stand. (Where exactly *do* our interests end, and our causes become the responsibility of others?) All the statement amounts to, in fact, is an instinctive reaction against any kind of political idealism. This is made explicit later in the essay, in similar terms of jocular cynicism: 'I think the best and most trustworthy political motive is self-interest. I share a widespread suspicion of the professional espouser of causes, the do-gooder, the archetypal social worker who knows better than I do what is good for me. . . .' This is not argument, but backchat. There is no logic in the writing; but there is self-revelation.

Amis reveals himself as a coward, too scared to take up any stand at all. Antagonistic to principles, he equates them with 'romanticism'—a word with good, pejorative overtones that he takes no trouble to define. At the same time he is careful to claim that he is himself a romantic, thus covering himself both ways. His humour is consistently derisive, of his own pretensions to seriousness as well as everyone else's: he will rather pose as a Philistine than run the risk of being despised as an intellectual— witness his meaningless crack about the 'alcoholic coma' of the intelligentsia. He can use no simple, emotional terms without apologizing for them ('Hopes and aspirations, to coin a phrase. . . .') He refuses to make his own position plain, referring throughout his pamphlet to 'our intellectual', 'your intellectual', 'our contemporary romantic', never explaining in what relationship he himself stands to this shadowy figure. And finally it is clear that he can only conceive of a cause in negative terms—in terms of war, or poverty or 'the rise of Fascism and so on . . .' (his own phrase). Socialism as a positive ideal, involving definable human values, apparently means nothing to him: his only real concern is not to be caught out, not to expose himself through naïf enthusiasm to the ridicule of the sophisticated, not to commit himself. One can only wonder why he continues to vote Left: through a lingering, irrational, shame-faced humanism, I suppose.

This humanism does not appear to be shared by John Wain, a writer whose name has been closely linked with Amis, and who has achieved a roughly equivalent celebrity in the same fashionable literary columns. As a result, when Wain explains his attitude to the contemporary situation, we find him implicitly far further to the right. I take this quotation from an article by him, 'How it strikes a Contemporary', from the *Twentieth Century* (the piece is carefully sub-headed '*A Young Man who is not Angry*'). The discussion is on education.

' Obviously the greatest single factor in keeping England a class-bound society is the fact that education is conducted along lines dictated by considerations of class. If you want to move towards a classless society, reorganize education. If you don't, leave it as it is. And the answer of the English people has always been quite unambiguous. They *don't* want a classless society. Only a few people here and there, mainly among the intelligentsia, certainly not 'normal' English folk, have ever wanted such a thing. Therefore, they don't want to reorganize education. The public schools remain, as part of a system of rewards. If you are 'successful', i.e. make money, one of the ways in which your success is rewarded is the power to send your children to expensive schools, where they will receive . . . the unalterable marks of membership of the governing class. Who am I to try to interfere with anything so deep-rooted?'

The attitude is essentially the same, with certain modifications. The disavowal of responsibility is complete and specific—though quite unargued. One might, after all, just as sensibly ask who is John Wain that he does *not* try to interfere with something so deep-rooted? It should all depend, of course, on what John Wain himself believes; but this we are not told. At least not in so many words. It is plain, however, where his sympathies lie, if only from the 'unambiguous' testimony which he cites so confidently on behalf of the English people ('English' is used for 'British' throughout the article); but just where this unmistakable answer has been given is not divulged. Notice again, too, the inferred denigration of the 'intelligentsia'—the cranky reformists—as opposed to 'normal' English *folk*.

Like Amis, Wain writes with a pretence of logical argument, but in fact he is doing little more than stating his preferences. They are conservative. Setting out, for instance, to justify 'The Establishment', he uses the odd reasoning that it deserves preservation because it has escaped the corruption which has vitiated popular culture and which therefore presumably disqualifies the people as a whole ('normal' English folk?) from serious regard. '. . . The life of a judge, a bishop, a professor, or a cabinet minister is substantially the same now as it was then (in the 1850's!). It follows that the traditionally English attitudes have survived best among these people. And this is no light matter.' What these traditionally English attitudes are, and how much they are worth, we are not informed; nor is there any suggestion that this privileged minority has any responsibility to other sections of the community. 'The working class have been robbed of their traditional way of life and, *until they have time to build up another*, they will be at the mercy of anything contemptuously thrown in their direction by the entertainment industry and the cheap press.' The italics are mine. The suggestion is thus that, until the working class has independently managed to accomplish this remarkable feat, we had better continue to side with 'the only people who have managed to get into any sort of relationship with the past . . . the property-owning aristocracy and *bourgeoisie* . . .' And this will involve, naturally, continued veneration for Eton and Winchester which, 'whatever else they may be and do, stand out as institutions with a conspicuously *national* flavour'.

The effect of such patent snobbery masquerading as reasoned argument is comic: but the spirit behind it is not. Writing like this is neither intellectually sharp nor morally sound; its statement amounts to little more in the end than a rationalized rejection of principle, a rejection of responsibility, and a disingenuous justification of the *status quo*. Amis's human impulses are genuine; even if he cannot really bring himself to trust them, he does not altogether abandon them either. Wain is talking already like an empty-headed, avuncular Tory:

'. . . That is why intelligence is the most crying need in English life today. And that intelligence must be directed towards the recovery of a national character, a 'way of life' that will revive national pride, in the best sense—the sort of pride that makes it impossible to stoop to meanness or bullying.'

At this rate he will soon be writing speeches for the Queen.

*   *   *

I have already stressed that what is important about Amis and Wain—in this context at least—is what they represent, the light their social and moral attitudes throw on the culture that has produced them, and made celebrities of them. I want to make this point clear, because otherwise I shall certainly be accused of personal malice. But ideas here are more interesting than personalities; and it is fascinating to see how completely, from the quotation of these two passages, the gaunt spirit of British 'liberalism' is conjured up.

I put 'liberalism' in inverted commas, because the genuinely liberal spirit is one which I respect, indeed do my best to express. But there is not much of it around in Britain at the moment. What we have in its place is a weak-limbed caricature, featuring only its most pallid virtues. This kind of liberal will commit himself to nothing more specific, or more dynamic, than a vague notion of 'decency'. He is on the humane side. He opposes the death penalty; he disapproves of our action in Suez. But his reactions are all *against*: his faiths are all negative. Tolerance is the most positive virtue he can accept, and for a political ideal he can find nothing more inspiring than the ambition 'not to find himself bossed around by a totalitarian government'—though this can hardly be more than a pious hope on his part, since he is mistrustful of political programmes, and does not really believe in the efficacy of political action. Politically, in fact, he exists in a vacuum, as Amis admits (though he implies, wrongly, that this is the inevitable position of a 'member of the intelligentsia', instead of simply a sad self-portrait). He is prepared to dislike, or deplore, particular phenomena in our society, as John Wain dislikes the entertainment industry and the cheap press, but he is not prepared to make connexions between abuses and the system which produces them. His paper is the *Observer*.

'The broad division of this country between Conservative and Labour (with a floating vote of ' liberals ') is not a division between good and bad, right and wrong (and this naturally goes for the ' liberals ' too, with whom this paper belongs). We believe that the two great political parties represent sections of the community that are of equally great merit; that there is equal value in the basic attitude, conservative and radical, which each represents.'

At first sight this quotation from an *Observer* editorial (for New Year, 1957) might appear to be an affirmation of a principle, a statement of mature Liberalism. That is obviously what was meant. But where (again) is the bloody horse? In fact affirmations of this kind amount to nothing more than a refusal to take the responsibility of analysing the situation in which we find ourselves today, and of agreeing on a consistent policy by which to deal with it. Effects remain unrelated to causes, and the *Observer*, which has consistently opposed Tory policy on such crucial issues as the death penalty, Cyprus and Suez, still continues to speak of the Right in benevolent general terms, and to find 'equal value' in its 'basic attitude'. This is not the maturity of liberalism, but its decay. All points of view are *not* equally right, and to suppose that it is somehow narrow-minded to opt for one consistent line of action rather than for all policies simultaneously is the shortest way to render oneself politically ineffective. With nothing to guide them but their kind hearts and their good intentions, liberals of this persuasion will probably be found on the progressive side of the barricades—but when the fight is already lost. They may charge the mounted police in Whitehall—but it will be at a demonstration that ought never to have been necessary. They will be conscientious objectors to wars which they have been too fair-minded to prevent.

There is no need to be an economist, or a political theorist, to understand that the world has changed, and that attitudes which sufficed a hundred years ago are not adequate today. Industrialism and mass education have transformed society, and crowded it to a point where everything impinges on, and affects, everything else. We can no longer afford the luxury of *laissez-faire*, and if we try, we are going to find that it is the most pernicious elements that come out on top. I have not got these ideas out of a book, nor from listening to the wireless, but from personal experience. I have learned that it is impossible to work in the cinema, or usefully to discuss it, without reference to the system within which films are produced; and once that reference is made, it is impossible not to consider the basis of the system, the way it has grown, the motives which sustain it and the interests that it serves. The kind of cinema it produces, and the kind of cinema it suppresses. And such considerations lead me inevitably to a political position. They do not make me a politician, nor a propagandist; but they give me direction. Naturally, they affect the way I look at things.

All this is extremely simple; and I am rather amazed that it should need to be said. But it is not only the 'liberals' who refuse to make these primary connexions. We find them equally shunned by intellectuals all along the Left, to whom art remains a diversion or an 'aesthetic experience', and Brecht is a bore. It is this, perhaps, as much as anything, which explains the deadness, the triviality, and ultimately the complete irrelevance of practically all the publicized art-work in this country at the moment. And in particular, of course, this applies to those channels of criticism and discussion, those disseminators of thought, the weekend reviews, the 'serious Sundays', and the critical programmes of the B.B.C. Right or Left here make no odds: it is a coterie world, perfectly directionless, a world of word-spinning and self-display, and it exists in a political limbo. (This is almost inevitable since the same people write in all the magazines.) From time to time gestures are made, allusions struck, which might seem to impinge on the outside world; but the only essential references are to other works of art, wine, or the personal foibles of the author. Ideas here have become totally dissociated from communal life, and the only audience considered worth addressing is the cultivated, 'liberal' few, who are flattered rather than discouraged by the implication that they belong to a minority.

' The Rest is Silence is a maddening novel, like a joke parcel, you go on unwrapping and find there is nothing really there . . . it leaves you feeling as if you had been turning over the pages of one of those unreadable magazines which you find in the lounges of Swiss hotels.'

'We are all existentialists nowadays, at least in the same vague, popular sense it was ever true to say we were all socialists. . . .'

'It was a great performance, but can I add—after being allowed to embrace Mme Feuillère figuratively and with infinite respect—that it was not the greatest conceivable performance? . . . I am almost sure I heard, with my own ears,

>Soleil, je te viens voir pour la dernier' fois.

Is it possible that Mme Feuillère could have missed one of the most beautiful e mutes in French literature? I prefer to think I had a momentary black-out. . . .'

It is surely preposterous that our leading radical weekly should address its readers in terms like these—for all three quotations are from the *New Statesman*, and none of them is parody. They illustrate perfectly what George Orwell, writing of the left-wing intelligentsia in *England their England*, described as their 'severance from the common culture of the country'; and they illustrate too (in their manner as much as their matter) how the cultural climate of the Left remains that of the *status quo*. This languid, over-sophisticated, salon voice is not one that could ever, conceivably, touch the conscience or inspire the heart to make new affirmations.

Some people may feel that this is unimportant; that culture and politics are unrelated. It is not, and they aren't. A socialism that cannot express itself in emotional, human, poetic terms is one that will never capture the imagination of the people—who are poets even if they don't know it. And conversely, artists and intellectuals who despise the people, imagine themselves superior to them, and think it clever to talk about the 'Ad-Mass', are both cutting themselves off from necessary experience, and shirking their responsibilities. Britain must be one of the few countries in the world where intellectuals are content to accept the bourgeois view of themselves as trivial *décorateurs*, or as irresponsible and anti-social outsiders. Or where artists insist on confining themselves to the manufacture of entertainment (more or less high-class) or to onanism, and lash out in angry fear when anybody suggests that their range might be extended if they could relate their work to the world outside themselves, or at least consider their art in relation to their fellow men. One knows that this raises complex problems, and nobody wants to impose a Zhdanovite socialist-realism here (the notion is more ludicrous than sinister); but it would do us no harm to at least start thinking about these things. Yet here, in 1957, is the reaction of an English poet to the suggestion that his work is likely to be impoverished if he continues to deny the relevance to it of the ideas of our time:

'Do these writers in any way justify the Soviet use of tanks and firing squads in Hungary? If they do not, it is strange that they fail to conclude that ideology is not necessarily a good thing. If they do, perhaps you will forgive a certain committedness in the expression if I say that their attitude seems to me to typify not 'the impassioned imaginative core' of our society, but a rapidly shrinking clique of intellectual and moral lepers.'

What is the significance of this hysterical refusal to take part in contemporary existence, to face its challenge and its risks? You would think our poets were sick, and perhaps they are—sick with the incurable, paralysing disease of mediocrity.

No doubt about it: we need a new intelligentsia just as much today as we did in 1941, when *England their England* was written. It is depressing indeed to find how little things have changed. A young writer like Amis will criticize Orwell (amongst other things, for encouraging 'political quietism'!), but he apparently fails to perceive how he, and his own generation, conform to the pattern of snobbishness and pusillanimity which Orwell exposed. The hope that the war might destroy these barriers, these inhibitions, has been proved vain: that sense of comradeship and mutual aid has vanished as though it had never been. To Amis himself now, any kind of direct relationship with working-people seems to imply unthinkable embarrassment, and he can only deal with it in facetious terms: 'I cannot see myself explaining, to an audience of dockers, say, just why homosexual relations between consenting adults should be freed from legal penalty.' I suppose this is meant to be funny; but what a disagreeable ignorance of what working-class people are really like. He ought to try the experiment he describes. He might be surprised to find that his own enlightenment is not so very much superior to that of the working-men—he might even get a good poem out of it.

* * *

We need, as I say, a new intelligentsia: and if we are not very careful, we are going to get one, though not of a kind that will do us much good.

'I would hardly count the Hungarian oppression or the Suez crisis as matters of supreme importance. They may involve 'human freedom', but after all, human freedom means a great deal more than political freedom, and I have always felt rather contemptuous of the sort of writer who allows himself to be swept into some political movement. It means he has committed himself too easily, too superficially.'

I have nothing against transcendentalism as such, or against religious faith: but I certainly mistrust it when it can achieve expression only in terms as egotistical, confused and anti-human in implication as Colin Wilson's doctrine of the neo-Superman. He is right to despise the 'liberal' intellectuals for their sapless, spineless triviality; but if they are merely rationalizing their own sense of defeat, he in his turn is only rationalizing his ambition, his conviction of superiority and his yearning for power. This is the swing-back of the pendulum with a vengeance—and nothing could be more ironic than the immediacy with which the liberal establishment collapsed under the first rude shove from the Outsider's elbow. Toynbee and Connolly went down on their knees, and within a week he was famous. A movement had been created. Significantly, the platform for the opinions I am quoting was given to Wilson by John Lehmann's post-post-Bloomsbury *London Magazine* (the review, it will be remembered, that Mr T. S. Eliot told us we had a moral obligation to buy).

'The writer is not merely to be blamed for standing apart in matters like the Hungarian revolution, and Rosenberg trial. If he is absolutely honest and really serious about the problems of his time, it is imperative that he stand apart. Any other attitude would open him to a charge of immaturity, jejeune [*sic*] silliness. . . . '

Again, it is not Wilson himself who matters, but the thought that we live in a society where the expression of a philosophy so immature, so jejune (and so, if I may say so, *jeune*) can elevate a young writer to instant celebrity. Is it really necessary to point out that even if human freedom, at its most metaphysical, means ' a great deal more than political freedom ', the two notions are not entirely separable? That a commitment to political principles need not necessarily be any more easy or superficial than a discipleship to Nietzsche or Shaw; and that to perceive the relationship between economic and human problems does not make a man a ' mere political jumping-jack '—another Wilsonian synonym for the man of social conscience.

Between the irresponsibility of this new authoritarianism, and the irresponsibility of the liberal sham, we have got to find our way : and perhaps the prospect is not as desperate as it looks. For at least certain myths, which have dominated and retarded us for far too long, have been lately exploded. The myth of the imperialist, hierarchic society has foundered at Suez and can never be raised again; and the myth of Russian-Communist infallibility, which for so many years absolved our left-wing intellectuals from the duty of thinking for themselves, has gone with the Twentieth Party Conference and the Russian action in Hungary. Are we to feel lost and deserted as a result? Or are we going to be capable of at last accepting our responsibilities to the present, and of finding political maturity? I started this essay with a despondent fantasy of the domestic scene. But it is not obligatory that the British intellectual should surrender to the pressures which would keep him, patronized and ineffective, in the nursery; nor is his only solution to escape. He could stay at home, grow up, and take over his inheritance.

If we are to do this, one of the first things we will have to learn is to talk to each other. This may seem an odd thing to say, when there is so evidently too much talk already; but I mean talk that relates to actuality, not just the incessant chasing of ideas round a wall of death. Useful controversy is something that is almost

F

impossible to achieve at the moment: discussion has become a game, in which there is general agreement that we should lay off personalities, that dog should not examine dog too closely, and speaking should not be frank. The result is a thick and airless atmosphere of common-room theorizing, in which to be too outspoken or specific is to be judged guilty of bad taste, or exhibitionism. The critical reception of *Look Back in Anger* was a good instance of this: of all the critics who attacked the play, how many were prepared to examine its implications with any degree of care? Another characteristic example of evasive action came from *The Times* not long ago—this time with reference to an article written by myself (on themes somewhat similar to those I have developed here):

'. . . [the article] certainly hits hard at those critics and that school of criticism Mr Anderson feels to be too recumbent, but it nevertheless gives the impression that it is an artificial exercise carried out for the purpose of testing the reactions of others, an elaborate trailing of the coat. . . .'

So your sincerity is doubted, or your integrity is accused; or you are patronized, or written off as an angry young man. And the embarrassing issues can continue to be evaded. Doubtless—it will be interesting to see—similar tactics will be used against this book. But I have a feeling they will be ineffective.

I have a feeling—and I hope it is more than a hope—that it is no longer seriousness that is felt to be a bore (particularly among younger people), so much as obsessional flippancy and the weary cult of the 'amusing'. When the *Universities and Left Review* appeared, in the spring of 1957, it was reviewed neither in the *New Statesman*, the *Observer*, the *Sunday Times*, nor *The Times*. Yet it sold out its first edition, reprinted, and sold out again. I take this as a portent. Perhaps people are beginning to understand that we can no longer afford the luxury of scepticism, that we must start again believing in belief. 'Only connect. . . .' said Forster, a long time ago; and it was a marvellously wise thing to say. But then, more recently, he told us that he did not believe in belief. Perhaps it is that that has muffled him. 'We had far better put our industry into being clever than into being good,' wrote V. S. Pritchett the other day in the *New Statesman*. The antithesis is not so much false, as old-fashioned.

Of course Lord Hailsham is right, and we must start being able to use words like duty, service, obligation and hope again without blushing—and community, and conscience, and love. But it is more than just a matter of bringing such terms back into fashion by using them in a party political broadcast. It is going to take a revolution to make these words clean, to revitalize the ideals they stand for, after their long debasement at the hands of journalists, politicians and copy-writers. And only a revolution of this kind can save us.

*   *   *

I may seem to have come a long way from the cinema : but the connexions are direct. In our country today, if you take a camera and lights into a factory, or a coal mine, or a market, there is always a time to go through in which the cry is ' J. Arthur Rank's here again!' 'Come on Clark Gable!' or 'Send for Diana Dors!' And this is not because the British are hopelessly self-conscious, or unimaginative, or facetious. It is because the cinema, as it is at present, can mean nothing to them except in terms of commercial parody. I want a Britain in which the cinema can be respected and understood by everybody, as an essential part of the creative life of the community. And if I have made a forty-minute film about the people of Covent Garden, I do not want to be told that I must cut it to eighteen minutes if I want British audiences to see it—because American feature films are running long this year. Those good and friendly faces deserve a place of pride on the screens of their country; and I will fight for the notion of community which will give it to them.

Fighting means commitment, means believing what you say, and saying what you believe. It will also mean being called sentimental, irresponsible, self-righteous, extremist and out-of-date by those who equate maturity with scepticism, art with amusement, and responsibility with romantic excess. And it must mean a new kind of intellectual and artist, who is not frightened or scornful of his fellows; who does not see himself as threatened by, and in natural opposition to, the philistine mass; who is eager to make his contribution, and ready to use the mass-media to do so. By his nature, the artist will always be in conflict with the false, the narrow-minded and the reactionary: there will always be people who do not understand the relevance of what he is doing: he will always have to fight for his values. But one thing is certain: in the values of humanism, and in their determined application to our society, lies the future. All we have to do is to believe in them.

A sense

of crisis

STUART HOLROYD

Stuart Holroyd

Born in Bradford, 1933. On leaving school decided against Oxford or Cambridge and took job as actor and assistant stage manager of local repertory company in Blackpool. Completed first full-length play at age of eighteen. It was based on the life of Thomas Chatterton. He calls it a ' wordy, poetic, incorrigibly romantic piece '. The play was not performed. Moved to London at age of nineteen. Planned to support himself by means of free-lance journalism, encouraged by the fact that he had already had some short stories and literary articles published. Finished his second play and translated a play from the French, but neither of these was performed. Married in 1954 and later that year, though continuing to write short stories and literary essays, took job as part-time secretary to Hugh Schonfield. 1955 : had essay on Rilke and Eliot published in *The Poetry Review*. Began writing a book studying the religious experience in six modern poets and its relation to their thought. In 1956, after various odd jobs, decided to study philosophy full time and obtained admission to University College, London, where, he says, he determined not to be influenced by the logical positivist views of Professor Ayer. *Emergence from Chaos*, his first book, published 1957.

I SUSPECT that all the great psychological concepts, the Freudian Oedipus Complex no less than the Nietzschean Will to Power, reflect the psychology of their originators. And for that reason, although I am not a professional psychologist, I have no hesitation in nominating the Will to Freedom as man's fundamental drive. I believe that it is the Will to Freedom that has motivated, unconsciously if not consciously, all that I have ever done; and I believe further that a properly directed Will to Freedom is the only thing that will save our civilization in its present hour of crisis.

One of the great mistakes of this century has been our persistence in seeking freedom on the political level. *Freedom is an inner condition.* It cannot be imposed from above, and it cannot exist in the community if it does not exist in the individual. Let me put my cards on the table at the start: I believe that his freedom is what characterizes the religious man, and consequently that the Will to Freedom in our time must express itself in a return to the religious attitude.

In my own experience, the Will to Freedom is not incompatible with the Will to Power. Indeed the two are inseparable, that is, provided it is understood that in Nietzsche, as in all religious men, the Will to Power took the self as its primary object. And the aspiring towards power over oneself is the same as the aspiring towards freedom. In fact, we might say that *freedom is power over oneself.*

Knowledge is power, and therefore it is in knowing himself that man attains to freedom. The formula 'Know thyself', when it was first introduced into the religion of the Greeks, constituted a great advance in civilization, a great step of liberation from primitive man's slavery to nature. One of the great faults of religion in our time is that it has tended to forget this formula.

People tell me that the religious revival I believe to be necessary is already taking place. But when I look for the signs of this supposed revival all I see is a widespread Billy Grahamism, a religion that makes its appeal to man's self-interest, taking for its slogan the words 'Get right with God', and which makes its converts by threatening them with hellfire and a judgement in the grand inquisitorial fashion. Only in a few of the artists and thinkers of our time do I see a healthy subjectivism, an absorption in self-knowledge for the sake of freedom.

Man is not born free—and the statement that he is is one of the great lies of our humanist culture. He is born an unfree, restricted, instinct-driven little animal, and he only really becomes man when, having conceived an idea of freedom, he strives to realize it within himself. And the 'within himself' is important, for the man whose idea of freedom consists in getting clear of his family or his creditors is obviously not willing for freedom in any profound sense of the word. Freedom, I repeat, is an inner condition. The free man is he who has a firm grasp on himself, a control over his faculties and his passions, an intellectual discrimination which liberates him from the thought habits of his time. He is, above all, the man who realizes that absolute freedom is a fiction, except for the insane, and that in fact freedom is defined as a condition of tension maintained between an aspiration and a limiting factor. In external freedom, the aspiration is towards gratification of one's own self-will and the limiting factor is responsibility to the society in which one lives. In the case of inner freedom the aspiration is towards a condition of union with God and the limiting factor is one's selfhood, one's physical being. The experience of these tensions broadens a man's grasp on existence, and it is precisely this breadth of grasp that is freedom.

Here, then, are three definitions of freedom which reduce to much the same thing: freedom consists in power over oneself, in self-knowledge, and in a broad grasp on existence. What they reduce to is the religious attitude. Now my argument is that the corruption of the religious attitude in our time has deprived man of his freedom, and has consequently deprived him also of his depth. Man has become trivial. He has become the slave of the manmade, and is carried around by the wheels of economic necessity which he himself set turning but is powerless to stop. From the nineteenth century and from the New World we have inherited a materialist standard of values. Inner freedom is on the whole discouraged, and we have substituted for it the myth of ' the free countries of the world ' which politicians so love to talk about. If a person has power, money, possessions, he is considered a worthy citizen. But take these things from him and what remains? A beast. What we call civilization is but a thin crust over the emptiness of our lives. Whether we live in a high-powered capitalist society, a welfare state or under a Communist totalitarianism, we are all threatened with the same fate: extinction of our individuality, increasing trivialization of our lives, and, consequent upon this, loss of relationship with anything beyond ourselves, alienation from God. In this situation only the religious attitude can restore to man his depth and his freedom.

In our time, therefore, the first thing that is required of a writer is a sense of crisis. He has a dual function to fulfil: to diagnose the sickness and to suggest the cure. It is not his business to ' mirror the age ', but to change it. He must get outside the age, view it in its historical perspective, discover when and how the process of degeneration started, and attack it at its roots. And the main root, he will find, is the humanist-scientific culture which has dominated the European scene for the last three hundred years, and infected all branches of thought, political, philosophical and aesthetic, with its poison. He will find, moreover, that the rational ' enlightened ' mind which this culture has produced will be the great obstacle that always stands in his way.

To this type of mind the beliefs of the religious man seem absurd and unfounded; the man of faith seems to have abdicated his position as a conscious human being. I used to hold these views myself when I was in my teens and had not yet liberated myself from my inherited humanist thought-habits. I see now that I was wrong. In my book, *Emergence from Chaos*, I have tried to follow through the psychological process which leads to faith. Religious faith, I now believe, is the highest condition of the soul, to be attained to only by means of patient and persistent self-discipline. The attainment of faith deepens a man's self-knowledge immeasurably.

That is what modern man needs: self-knowledge. He needs to know himself as determined eternally as well as temporally, in relation to transcendence as well as in relation to the world. The necessary precondition of all knowledge is wakefulness. Most men are asleep and need to be wakened up. One of the artist's first tasks is to shake the foundations of man's complacency, to awaken him to a realization of his own imperfection. Self-knowledge is deepened by self-division. The man who is divided against himself learns more about his own essential nature than the man who conducts his existence pretty steadily upon one level. The psychologist or philosopher who has not been through an experience of acute inner division is ill-equipped for his job. He is like a man who goes to break up a road with a hammer instead of a pneumatic drill. He lacks the power, the energy, to drive deep down into his subject. Electric power is only produced when you effect a contact between a positive and negative pole. The analogy holds on the psychological level. It is by dividing himself against himself and by striving always to become an unified whole, that a man generates power within himself. And it is this power born of division that produces works of art, and inspires progress in psychology, philosophy and the sciences.

The ancients realized this truth. Herakleitos was the first to formulate it. He regarded existence as ' an attunement of opposite tensions ', and believed strife to be the fundamental law of nature. The Church Fathers took over the idea. The notion of the existence of Heaven and Hell and of the conflict between God and Satan, is a projection into myth of the psychological experience of the divided man. In our time—and the decline of religious faith is responsible for this—division has come to be regarded as a disease, rather than as the necessary condition of human, as distinct from animal, existence. We label the divided man a psychopath, and pack him off to the psycho-analyst to be ' put right '. And the pity is that the treatment is usually effective, because the patient was not really divided at all. He had contracted a little neurosis, as a result, perhaps, of repression, or even just overwork. Nothing that couldn't be put right after a few ten-guinea consultations! Nothing to prevent him being easily reassimilated into the old routine! Psycho-analysis certainly fulfils a useful function in our high-powered society. But it is a phenomenon produced by civilization at a certain stage of its development, an off-shoot and not an integral part of the main structure. We can conceive society progressing to the stage when all the psycho-analysts would be out of work. The view of man implicit in most modern psychology (that of Jung is the notable exception) is superficial, and materialist to the core. When the care of man's psychic life passed from the hands of the priest into those of the scientifically trained specialist something very important was lost: the realization that division is not a disease, but is radical in man, and is what distinguishes him as a spiritual being.

The first task of any serious writer in our time, therefore, must be to galvanize people into wakefulness, to broaden their grasp on existence by making them aware of their own divided nature. It is his job to graft a new dimension on to human existence, give it a new depth, for this is the only way to freedom. If we do not make ourselves free before long, if we do not wake up and deepen existence, it is going to be too late, and we'll find ourselves picking up the pieces and wondering how to put them together again. Waking up consists first of all in waking up to oneself (religious awakening), and only secondarily in waking up to the world (political awakening). This should always be the sequence: first organize yourself, and only then consider yourself sufficiently mature to attempt to organize the society.

In practice we rarely find that the people who govern are religiously awakened individuals. The myths of democracy and representative government have placed the controls in the hands of arbitrarily chosen individuals who, more often than not, have no ideas about the very delicate art of governing. They scramble along short-sightedly from one problem to another, solving them as best they may, and are genuinely surprised when they find themselves involved in a war or an economic depression. The democratic principle has by now rooted itself firmly in the Western world and it is difficult to conceive how the situation could be changed; but an observer of post-war developments in the United States cannot help noticing how democracy tends towards totalitarianism, albeit a more benevolent form of totalitarianism than is practised in present-day Russia and her satellite countries. It may be that in a world which is split down the middle, and in which power is the end to which all else is sub-jugated, totalitarianism is inevitable. But we must have gone wrong somewhere to find ourselves in this situation.

One of the fundamental mistakes, I believe, was that of believing in the efficacy of a system of representative government. Such a system is a myth. No man can represent another. All he can do is represent his interest. And when government is based upon interests, the larger, more important political issues are lost sight of. The problem of how to ensure the greatest possible degree of inwardness in the individual members of the community and still maintain social cohesion, is a political one. For when a people lacks inwardness it lacks vision, lacks foresight. And even if we conceive politics as a purely prudential affair, having no object but the survival of the community, we must admit that a community which lacks foresight is in a very precarious situation. This is the kind of problem that the system of representative government is ill-equipped to solve, or even to consider. The alternative is to acknowledge that government is an art which should be in the hands of an expert minority, and at the same time to make the system fluid enough to prevent power falling into the hands of self-interested demagogues. If the minority are fully matured men, i.e. individuals who have awakened religiously, they will have two faculties which, if they could be made effective on the political level, would have profound and revolutionary repercus-sions: deep psychological insight and a developed moral sense. The first of these would operate to ensure better conditions within the community, the second would ensure more harmonious relations between communities. The example of the greatest civilizations of the past bears out my point: for they were all hierarchical.

It may seem vain to attack so firmly established an institution as that of representative government. But I am not here campaign-ing for a political revolution. All I am trying to do is to point out how certain characteristic features of our society—the growth of psycho-analysis, the democratic principle in the government, the faith in progress, the triumph of rationalism over religion—all imply a view of the nature of man which is at bottom superficial.

Man is not wholly determined from below, but also, and more essentially, from above. He is not only a social or political animal, a mere member of the crowd. He is also an eternally existing individual who stands absolutely responsible for his actions before God. Most modern men have lost the feeling of their uniqueness, and have consequently become alienated from God. It is commonly believed that science has made God an anachronism. But the truth of the matter is that man has become so trivial that he no longer feels the existence within himself of anything that would be worthy of God's interest. Belief in immortality has also waned, not because it has been disproved scientifically, but because man no longer sees any reason why he *should* be immortal. What is most urgently required at the present time is that men should recover a sense of their uniqueness, and should, with all their power, *will* to be immortal. It is no exaggeration to say that survival depends upon this.

I believe that the writers and the philosophers can do a great deal in this situation. Indeed, I believe that because they are (presumably) men conscious of the predicament, the responsibility for doing it devolves upon them. They can :

(a) make men more aware and awake (shock tactics here permitted),

(b) preserve values (that is, maintain their integrity in spite of everything—a positive, but nevertheless a static rôle),

(c) vigorously re-define values (the philosopher's task),

(d) instead of showing what man is, show what he can become (the dramatist's and fiction-writer's task).

It is the distinction of Bernard Shaw that he succeeded in doing all four of these things. Various other writers have been active in one way or another. This activity now needs to be stepped up. We need a generation of writers and thinkers who combine intellectual vigour and clear-sightedness with artistic capacity, imagination and creativeness. At the moment of writing I do not know what the other contributors to this book will have to say, but I am confident that certain of them will show that they belong to this category.

Our present need is not so much to come back to religion as to re-discover and re-create it. That is the task we must set ourselves.

The majority of people have lost all conception of what religion is about. Recently I was in an Odeon cinema on a Sunday. Slipped into the programme (unadvertised) was a short called *A Thought for Today*—three minutes of maudlin moralizing. I asked the manager who made these films, and told him I thought them an insult to the audience's intelligence. He explained that J. Arthur Rank is 'a very keen Methodist', and said I was the first person he had known complain about the films. Most people, I suppose, consider them edifying and put up with them as a sort of concession to religion. And J. Arthur Rank enjoys the nice warm feeling of the do-gooder. I don't doubt that he makes the films in good faith. But this advertising of supposedly fine sentiments as if they were some new kind of breakfast cereal just demonstrates what I mean when I say that most people today have no conception of what religion is about. The crowd-drawing power of Billy Graham and other cavaliers of the Cross is yet another sign. And the fact that the Church approves of Graham's methods, and has even worked out a follow-up system in conjunction with him, finally clinches my point. Religion needs to be completely overhauled and re-defined. A number of individuals need to come to the fore who are genuine religious men, who have thought and felt deeply, and are capable of teaching by their example what the religious life really is.

The obstacles which prevent the average modern man from ever attaining to the religious attitude are numerous. Three centuries of humanist culture have bequeathed us a burden of ideas and attitudes which few people ever get around even to questioning, and which are quite incompatible with the religious attitude. Liberalism, the dogma of equality, the faith in scientific method, the myth of progress and the idea of the perfectibility of man, may be cited as examples. We all grew up in the climate of these ideas, and it is difficult for us to shake ourselves free of them. But we must, somehow, if we are to survive as anything more than a race of ingenious little animals.

The popular misconceptions of the nature of religion which are so common in our time are nearly all traceable to the same fundamental mistake. People confuse the religious attitude with its consequences. They transfer the emotions which it is proper they should feel for the religious man to the actions which they believe to be characteristic of him. Religion thus becomes loving your neighbour, doing good works, being tolerant or charitable. If questioned about it, people would no doubt admit that there is a certain state of the soul which is prior to these actions and of which they are the expression, but as a rule it is the actions they have in mind when they speak of religion, and not the fundamental attitude out of which they proceed. In other words religion has lost its inwardness. And that means that it has become nothing, for religion without inwardness is unthinkable. People must be made to realize that the patterns of behaviour which have come to be thought characteristic of the religious man are by no means inevitable. A man may be uncharitable, intolerant and self-centred, and still be profoundly religious. The kernel of the religious life is what I have called the religious attitude. Instead of wasting our emotions of reverence on various incidental fruits of this attitude, we should labour to understand it and to realize it within ourselves. Such understanding brings a depth of psychological insight which most men seem to be afraid of. They have reason to be. It is an insight which shakes the foundations of life and requires us completely to re-orient our lives—a most inconvenient thing to have to do.

However, I believe such a radical re-orientation to be absolutely necessary at the present time. Man needs to understand himself more profoundly in order to live more humanly, that is, on more than one level. And it is the writer's job to make him so understand himself. In *Emergence from Chaos* I have tried to define the religious attitude and to trace its genesis. In my next two books (of which I shall speak later) I am setting out to study in more detail the psychology of that attitude in its various manifestations, and thus at once to broaden and deepen the definition of religion by returning to its dynamic centre in the human psyche.

This is where our work of re-creating religion must begin: in our own innermost being. Compared with us, the evangelists are like a quack doctor who applies a lotion to the body in order to cure a deep-rooted inner disease. They fail to get to the root of the matter. Our method must be that of the skilled surgeon. With complete objectivity we must dissect our experience, mercilessly criticize ourselves, until we are utterly free from the illusions with which life in the world fetters us. We must gain access to that dynamic centre which is within all of us, though dormant in most, and set it working at full pressure. We must learn again, and practise, those disciplines which religious men in all ages and of all persuasions have found effective in liberating those deeper energies which most men do not even suspect that they possess.

In 1906 William James wrote an essay, *The Energies of Men*, in which he advocated the study of what he called 'dynamo-genesis', that is, of the sources and limits of human power. In the same year he gave an address to the Harvard Psychology Club in which he outlined his ideas about 'functional psychology'. This branch of the subject, he said, should study those energies which operate in man's religious life, and seek to work out a technique for their development and control. James, like another eminent physiologist, Dr Alexis Carrel, believed in the possibility of science effecting a 'remaking of man'. The latter, in his book *Man, the Unknown* (1935), carried James's work forward, and laid the foundations for the development of a comprehensive science of man. Another thinker who had meanwhile been working on similar lines was the German psychologist and philosopher, Karl Jaspers. Jaspers later spoke of his psychology as *Existenz Clarification*. He explained, 'This psychology was no longer merely an empirical statement of the facts and laws of events. It was an outline of the potentialities of the soul which holds a mirror up to man to show him what he can be, what he can achieve and how far he can go.'

All these three scientific thinkers were profoundly religious men. They were the pioneers of an attitude which must become more widely held in our time, and they laid the foundations for the work which it is the responsibility of the writer of my generation to continue. What they had in common was a faith in man's ability to change himself; and what they all implied was that *if he does not change himself he must inevitably perish*.

People are always talking about the historical process and the patterns of decline and fall in civilizations as if these were inexorable natural laws quite beyond the control of the human will. One thing they do not seem to take into account is that our civilization is scientifically more advanced than any previous one, and we thus have an unprecedented knowledge of the causes of its decay. Modern Man has his salvation in his own hands in a way that the members of previous civilizations did not have. We can diagnose our sickness, and that is the first step to curing it. It is conceivable that by a supreme effort of will at the present time we could attain to a higher form of civilization than has ever been known on the earth.

The problem is, of course, how to employ the will. The 'rebel without a cause', the man with plenty of will but no direction, has become a stock figure of contemporary literature. We must be careful to distinguish between the defiant will and the religious will. The will power of the religious man is generated, so to speak, in a continuous stream from the dynamic centre within. That of the 'rebel without a cause' expresses itself in outbursts of petulance, is essentially negative, and is a less integral part of the man's character. Men possessing a defiant will always seem to arise when a civilization is on its last legs. In the last days of both the Greek and Roman cultures the philosophical schools of the Stoics made their appearance. Sartre, Camus and certain of the other French existentialists are, of course, the great Stoics of our day. The 'rebel without a cause' does not have the dignity of the Stoic, however. Stoicism is the last outpost in the retreat from faith, where the human spirit takes its stand and firmly asserts the validity of human values. It is thus distinguished from mere rebellion in being defiantly positive instead of defiantly negative.

Stoicism is a sort of Siren's song for the thinking man in our age. It is a most seductive philosophical attitude, because it has at its centre a profound and compelling truth: the truth that man makes himself, and by virtue of his actions in the world shapes a self which did not exist before and which constitutes the whole justification of his existence. Like the authentic religious attitude, this view places the emphasis on the efficacy of the will, but essentially it is philosophy with its back to the wall. It leads to an extreme subjectivism, to the individual nursing his own salvation and saying, Let the rest of the world go hang! It implies a denial of the existence of any communal purpose for mankind, and thus it can make no contribution to the work of salvaging a civilization. The presence of God in a philosophical system has the effect of making it fluid and comprehensive and alive. When God is dropped out, philosophy stiffens into stoicism. In the past, stoicism has proved to be the last outburst of human greatness in a civilization that was about to relapse into barbarism. The challenge of our time, in so far as it presents itself in philosophical terms, is to resist the Siren's song of stoicism, transcend it, and thus enter upon a new age of religious faith.

For most modern men, stoicism will be a stage on the way to faith. When a man awakens to consciousness of our crucial historical situation and of his own personal responsibility, he must confront the problem of how he should employ his will. And his first answer should be: in deepening his inwardness, his self-knowledge. It is here that the rebellious types go wrong. Instead of entering into themselves they vainly kick against the pricks. I have said before that a man must awaken to himself before he awakens to the world, and this period of self-absorption is likely to produce a stoical attitude to life. This attitude is a great advance from the condition of semi-consciousness in which most people live, and the further step which turns the stoic into a man of faith comes fairly naturally when he is made to consider the consequences of his position.

This, at least, was my own experience. I passed from total scepticism through a kind of stoicism, and emerged into belief. I venture to generalize the experience partly because I have observed a similar pattern of development in people of my acquaintance and also in certain contemporary literary figures, and partly because I believe that my starting point was typical of that of the majority of men today.

My home background, in so far as it was religious at all, was methodist. I soon revolted against the sloppy thought-habits and the sentimental ethic of this lowest branch of Protestantism, and declared myself an atheist. The first awakening of anything that could be called a religious sense in me was caused by my reading of the Romantics—particularly Keats and Wordsworth. I thought that the vague sense of the infinite which they communicated was an adequate substitute for the ridiculous belief in God. I subscribed to the religion of art, and was seduced by the aesthetes.

I became proud of my humanism, and thought myself 'enlightened'. Then I read Dostoevsky, and Berdyaev's book on Dostoevsky, and William James's *Varieties of Religious Experience*. I read all these together during an illness, and on reflection I came to realize that I had been intellectually ill for years, constipated with a bundle of ideas and attitudes that were not my own but which I had unquestioningly adopted because they were a part of my cultural inheritance. I realized then that humanism—at least the kind of humanism that was atheistic and set itself up as a substitute for religion—was a diseased attitude which had produced a race of spiritually stunted men. The discussions between Alyosha and Ivan Karamazov about the existence of God and the meaning of good and evil seemed far more real and vital to me than the laborious discussions of the ethics of social acts that I had been accustomed to hearing and partaking in. A new dimension of existence was opened up to me and at the same time a new power born within.

So my first approach to religion was psychological. I saw that certain states of mind, certain faiths passionately held, invested life with a deeper significance, and afforded man a more penetrating vision of his own nature and that of the world, than any rational or philosophical approach to these questions could ever obtain. I saw also that the religious life fostered certain virtues in men which I valued highly: creativity, self-abnegation, energetic singleness of purpose, intellectual vigour and power of will. Religion was simply life at its highest pitch of intensity, and for that reason alone it was man's more authentic level of existence. When a man lives intensely, the question of the reasonableness of belief becomes a trivial one, for he knows that it is not reason that is essential to life, but will.

To live intensely means to live consciously. And the mark of conscious living is that it is oriented towards the future. The more distant the future, the greater degree of consciousness is required to grasp it as a *telos*. When the future is conceived as being beyond life, i.e. when life is oriented towards immortality, then you get what might properly be called religious existence.

It was with these basic ideas in mind that I embarked upon my first book, *Emergence from Chaos*. Chaos is the unconscious. It is his attempt to emerge further and further from the animal condition of unconscious existence that distinguishes man as a spiritual being. I traced this psychological development through six modern poets; taking Dylan Thomas as the least conscious, and T. S. Eliot as the most conscious, of the six. The book was thus a sort of literary *Varieties of Religious Experience* with a dogmatic point to it. The scheme which determined the choice of poets and the order of their appearance was a psychological one, and it reflected the pattern of my own experience. The idea of division, about which I have already spoken, was central in it. Both Yeats and Rimbaud were divided men, and for me their inner conflicts illuminated the human condition as determined religiously in a way that the writings of the poets of assured faith could not do. Inner division heightened a man's consciousness. It was the struggle between consciousness and faith that generated the most highly charged creative energy. The sacrifice of reason was the most passionate act a man could perform. It was, paradoxically, the mark of his freedom.

The problems of consciousness and freedom are, of course, problems of philosophy. But when I turned to the philosophers I found that, with a few exceptions, they had no interest in the problems as they presented themselves to my mind. For them they were not problems of existence, having a profound bearing upon their own personal lives, but mere problems of analysis with which they occupied themselves only in the hours when they were philosophizing. I found the whole tradition of philosophy since Descartes antipathetic to my own temperament and beliefs. The definition of the philosopher as the man who doubts everything, seemed to me quite wrong. The philosopher should surely be the man of faith, the man of vision. I resolved to do all in my power to shake the security of the philosophical school of linguistic analysis which still predominates in English and American universities. I felt that what was lacking in the English intellectual climate was the sense of crisis; not so much of political crisis, but rather of the more fundamental crisis in human existence. People were not conscious of the fact that man was gradually being reduced in stature, and the range of his emotional life steadily narrowed down. This must be made clear to them.

What was needed in England was an existentialist literary-philosophical movement.

No philosophy that is satisfied with man as he is is worthy of the name. The true philosophy demands imperatively that man *be* more. It issues a warning and a challenge. It turns a man's eyes inward upon himself, upon his soul, and reveals, more often than not, that he possesses neither self nor soul. Be great, or perish : that is its warning. Possess yourself, realize yourself, develop yourself : that is its challenge. It points to the *higher potential* in human existence, to authentic being. It casts the ideal of human life beyond human life, and requires man to orient himself in relation to that ideal. Philosophy is not adequately defined as analysis : it is a drive towards deeper self-knowledge, towards greater power over oneself and over nature, towards more life, for life consists in power.

To the logical positivist philosophers this will sound like heresy. But to my mind it is they who have swallowed the greatest heresy of modern times : that of the supremacy of science and scientific method. The end of science is to advance knowledge. The primary end of philosophy is not knowledge, but life. Man can do without knowledge, but he cannot do without action. His first need is to live purposively and intensely. And philosophy, by illuminating the various levels of existence and pointing to its *telos* or end, enables him to do this.

We can distinguish three kinds of philosophy : epistemology, which asks How can I know?—metaphysics, which asks What can I know?—and existential philosophy, which asks How can I live more? how plug into the vital current of life and thus exist more really, more intensely? It is because they ignore these latter questions that most modern professional philosophers have become mere co-workers with the scientist, analysers of scientific terms. But a philosophy into which the philosopher's own reality does not enter is a shadowy thing. Produced by men without selves and without profundity, it can have neither substantiality nor significance for a man who wills to apprehend himself on that level of his being where he enters into his relationship with the transcendent.

The philosophy which ultimately counts must be conscious of

itself in its historical situation. The contemporary situation has produced the supposedly rival philosophies of existentialism and logical positivism, the one being eminently historically conscious and the other not at all so. But the modern world will tolerate no neutrals. You are either involved in the degenerative process of civilization, or you set yourself apart and resolutely oppose it. What unites the so-called existentialists is their realization of this degenerative process, though their opposition to it takes different forms. But the logical positivists are blind to it—as philosophers, I mean, not as men (but who knows what they think as men, since they never deign to tell us?). Bertrand Russell is of course the exception, but he states emphatically that his writings on politics, sociology and morality have nothing to do with his philosophical activity. This narrowing down of the scope of philosophy is churlish, and has no historical justification. Philosophy arises whenever you get a man thinking about his own essential nature and his relation to the universe; professional philosophy when you get a highly sophisticated man excogitating over refinements of this fundamental problem.

Positivism is well defined in W. B. Yeats's lines about 'Whiggery':

> A levelling, rancorous, rational sort of mind
> That never looked out of the eye of a saint
> Or out of a drunkard's eye.

Yeats's use of the word 'levelling' here recalls Kierkegaard's indictment of the 'levelling process' which he foresaw would lead to the despiritualization of man. Auguste Comte's positivism, his 'Religion of Humanity' and celebration of 'the divine average', advanced this process; and it was on foundations established in part by Comte that the Viennese Circle—the group of philosophers who formulated logical positivism in 1928—based their philosophy. Positivism is the philosophy of a civilization which the myth of equality has taken by the throat. It abhors individualism. It reduces man to a function and strips him of his essential humanity. In ethics it produces utilitarianism, in psychology a naïve empiricism. It distrusts the faculties of imagination and intuition, and will be guided only by the light of reason. The positivist philosopher is a modest fellow. He is not conscious of any high vocation, and if you ask him how a man should conduct his life or attain the greatest possible fullness of life, he will be embarrassed and refer you to the clergyman or the psycho-analyst. The greatest passion he knows is the passion for truth, but for him truth is synonymous with correctness, exactitude. The great insoluble questions that have troubled mankind since the dawn of consciousness he lumps together as metaphysical and consequently nonsensical, and consigns to the dust-bin. In short, he lacks vision. He is just another mediocrity in a world of mediocrities, a world which is slowly committing suicide, suffocating itself with the myths of equality and progress. He does not, or will not, realize that the function of the philosopher in our time is not to describe the limits of knowledge, but to show man what he can become.

A French existentialist was asked what he thought of a logical positivist's penetrating critique of his ideas. He replied: 'He is a cow!' When the situation is reversed and the existentialist becomes the critic, the logical positivist is equally unmoved, and says that the former is illogical and emotionally biased. The lack of any common ground between the two has reduced criticism to abuse, and in Western Europe at the present time two insular philosophies confront each other, each unable to contribute anything to the other's development because temperamentally the thinkers of both schools are worlds apart. This is regrettable, for the great philosopher of the future will have to combine the positive elements in both schools. He will have to have both the intellectual rigour and the clarity of the logical positivist, and the depth of vision and psychological acuteness of the existentialist. My own sympathies and temperamental bias place me emphatically on the side of the existentialists, but, being a thinker of a later generation, and consequently unattached to either school, I cannot but recognize that by clearing away a good deal of philosophical dead wood the analytical philosophers will have done the creative thinkers of the future a useful service. Socrates was the existential thinker *par excellence*, but in him the critical and analytical faculty was highly developed. So it was also in Alfred North Whitehead, a philosopher of our time who, because he stands between the two schools, has not been sufficiently appreciated by either. Throughout the history of philosophy the visionary temperament has been in conflict with the analytical, the mystical with the rational. It is when this conflict has been waged within one man that the really great philosophies have been produced, when depth has been allied with lucidity, and comprehensiveness augmented by vision. In the twentieth century this conflict has ceased to be subjective and creative, however, and has occasioned a cold war between two schools. The most urgent need in philosophy at the present time is that the conflict should be restored to the subjective level.

In philosophy, as in art and many other departments of life, no progress is made except by virtue of the creative tension in which those few people live whose minds are capable of grasping and holding on to the polarities of existence. 'Progress' is, of course, an equivocal term, and the disciple of Russell will contradict me and say that progress is only possible through the efforts of a number of scientifically-minded philosophers who resolve to 'divide and conquer' the problems of philosophy and are content to work slowly towards the truth by means of hypothesis and experiment. I reply that such progress, which involves reducing man to a mere function in the interests of 'knowledge', is the most pernicious myth of our time. The only real progress possible today is a general deepening of inwardness. Philosophy is not a science. The philosopher who prides himself on being a 'disinterested seeker after truth' is a ridiculous figure, for the essential precondition for the apprehension of truth is interestedness, involvement in the flux of existence. Scientific method in philosophy can lead to the discovery of new facts. But fact is not truth. Truth itself (as distinct from truth *about* something, which is fact) is a condition of living. No amount of thinking will enable me to apprehend truth, unless I bend all my efforts to the task of *living in truth*. And living in truth is living dynamically in a condition of tension. *I must root the polarities of existence firmly in my consciousness for my only way of attaining to truth is through them.*

This is my most fundamental belief. It could perhaps be reduced to banal terms by saying that the philosopher must be a well-balanced individual. I would not mind that, provided it were understood that the extremes between which the philosopher has to maintain his equilibrium are infinitely wider than those which determine the normal man. If we envisage existence as extended between the poles, say, of hopeless despair and ecstatic affirmation of life, with a series of relative poles proceeding inwards from the extremes to the centre where the existential subject stands, then we have a measure for the greatness of man, for he is greatest whose grasp encompasses the widest extent of existence, and who, though he may vacillate between one extreme and the other, ultimately finds his equilibrium in a condition of dynamic tension. In the philosopher this tension often takes the form of a conflict between reason and vision, intellect and intuition. The resolution of this conflict results in the atrophy of the mind and the loss of one's grasp on reality. The attempt to resolve it, however, is the very condition of creativity; for man is most creative, and therefore most fully himself, when inner conflict has brought consciousness to its highest pitch of intensity.

Creativity is one of the touchstones of greatness in my conception of philosophy. Inwardness is the other. In creativity and in inwardness man realizes himself as spirit and transcends himself as creature. This, and no other, is the ultimate purpose of life. The philosopher who is neither creative nor possesses himself in inwardness is a fraud, a mediocrity. It is the creative thinker who, however diverse his insights may be, and however confused his expression, advances the spiritual evolution of mankind. If he does not confine himself within the limits of official philosophy, that is no reason why we should decline to call him a philosopher. He extends those limits. He makes philosophy what it should be: a comprehensive science of man.

It is not surprising that the creative thinker should turn to the novel and the drama as media of expression more suitable than the academic treatise. His business is not analysis, but the communication of a sense of life. His purpose is not to divert or exercise his reader's intellect, but to awaken him to an awareness of the dramatic nature of existence, the perilousness of human life, the delusion of all ideas of security, in order that he might begin to live more authentically, to spend his life, as Unamuno says, so that he might deserve to be immortal. For the fulfilment of such a purpose the novel and the drama are the ideal vehicles of expression. The essence of existence is drama. Man attains his highest through conflict. In the fiction of Dostoevsky, Kafka and some of the modern existentialists, discoveries have been made which are as significant as any arrived at by means of psycho-analysis, the microscope or the mathematical equation. The novel can thus be at once a means of imaginative psychological research and a vehicle for indirect moral exhortation. Literature and philo-sophy are only separate activities of the human mind in their lower forms. Both are creative activities, and the highest literature is philosophical in its implications, just as the highest philosophy is literary in its expression.

Most of the fiction and drama which has been produced in this country since the war has been trivial. Sensitivity and charm have become the criteria of excellence in the absence of those qualities which make great literature, namely, energy, vision and power. The novels and plays which have been taken most seriously are those expressing a mood of hopelessness, futility and impotence. No doubt it is the mood of the age, but that mood, I hope the reader of these pages will now see, is symptomatic of contem-porary man's unfreedom. He feels himself to be impotent and futile precisely because he lacks freedom, and he lacks freedom because he lacks inwardness, depth, breadth of grasp on existence. The writers who express this mood no longer retain even the sense of crisis which the writers of the thirties and forties, Orwell, Malraux, Huxley, Koestler, Hemingway, etc., possessed. Their works certainly reflect the crisis, but they do not seem to be conscious of it in the way these earlier writers were. And yet a sense of crisis is one of the first things needful in the writer today. He must see the crisis of our time as a threat to human freedom, and must seek to restore freedom in the only way possible : by deepening inwardness and, by means of his psycho-logical vision, extending the limits of consciousness.

It is important to distinguish between the vision of absurdity of certain of the contemporary French writers and the sense of futility of their English counterparts. The difference between these two is the most important in the world, for it is the difference between life in a condition of dynamic tension and life which is oriented to only one of the poles of existence, and has therefore lost its intensity and its meaning. The characters in the English novels and plays which I have in mind are of this latter type. They have let go of life. They are fundamentally different from Camus' '*l'homme absurde*', who realizes that he must live by virtue of the absurd, and that if he commits actual or intellectual suicide he does not triumph over the absurd (as Dostoevsky's Kirillov imagined), for it disappears with his act and meaninglessness supervenes. The vision of absurdity is one of the poles of existence. Its correlate is the pole of reason and the will to live. So long as a man maintains his hold on these two poles he completes the circuit, so to speak, and the vital force of life flows through him. If he releases his hold he becomes nothing, or—which is much the same thing—the hero of a best-seller.

I have said that my most fundamental belief is that my only way to truth and to freedom is by way of rooting the polarities of existence firmly in my consciousness. This defines the purpose of all my literary activity. All my work is founded upon the psychological premise that through and in conflict with himself man attains to the greatest fullness of life, to authentic existence, to the optimum development of his consciousness, in fact to freedom. Division was, as I have already said, central in the psychological plan of *Emergence From Chaos*. In my next two books I propose to study the most frequent cause of division, i.e. despair, and its most extreme expression: demonism.

Despair and demonism are, I believe, the most important and the most characteristic subjects of literary psychology in all the literature of the nineteenth and twentieth centuries. My two books (the first called *The Dialectics of Despair* and the second provisionally entitled *The Mark of Cain*) will trace the variations played upon these themes in literature from the Romantics to the present day. Their development will be psychological, however, not chronological. My primary purpose is not to write a study in literary history, but to show how despair and demonism may be respectively the starting point for, and an expression of, the religious attitude. I have also a subjective purpose in writing these books: that of orienting myself within existence and in my historical situation. The last chapter of *The Dialectics of Despair* will be called *The Despair of Europe.* It will be a further attempt to diagnose the sickness of our age. In my diagnosis of this sickness I believe that I point to what in my opinion is the only possible cure: the religious attitude. In these pages I have been occupied in trying to define this attitude, to show how it is arrived at and what beliefs characterize it.

A friend of a slightly older generation expressed surprise—I think he was even a little amused—that I should be able with such apparent confidence to plan for the future. The feeling that there is no future is very common today, particularly among the generation who were in the last war and feel that somehow they missed their chance after it—their last chance. Certainly the future prospect is not one conducive to optimism. But it is equally certain that by lapsing into tensionless pessimism we make things worse. As I conceive it, the duty of the writer and thinker in our time is to work on the hypothesis of a future, and to show the conditions necessary for authentic existence. His first task is to make men aware, to awaken them to realities. And human life becomes real only when it establishes a relationship with transcendence. The philosopher must therefore concern himself not only with the future of mankind as a whole, i.e. the social problem, but also with the future of the individual in his eternal aspect: the religious problem. He must be a religious thinker.